# PROGRAMMING
*with*
# PURPOSE

**Other Student Impact Resources**

Student Ministry for the 21$^{st}$ Century
Impact Sports
Small Group Resources, vol. 1: Walking with Christ
Small Group Resources, vol. 2: Compassion for Lost People
Small Group Resources, vol. 3: Learning to Serve
Small Group Resources, vol. 4: A Lifelong Calling
Life-Changing Camps and Retreats

# STUDENT IMPACT

# PROGRAMMING

*with*

# PURPOSE

DEVELOPING

A PROCESS

FOR

PROGRAMMING

# TROY MURPHY

*With Kim Anderson*

ZondervanPublishingHouse
*Grand Rapids, Michigan*

*A Division of HarperCollinsPublishers*

WILLOW CREEK RESOURCES

*Programming with Purpose*
Copyright © 1997 by the Willow Creek Association

Requests for information should be addressed to:

## ZondervanPublishingHouse
*Grand Rapids, Michigan 49530*

---

**Library of Congress Cataloging-in-Publication Data**

Murphy, Troy.
    Programming with purpose : developing a process for programming / Troy Murphy with
Kim Anderson.
        p.  cm.
    Includes bibliographical references.
    ISBN: 0-310-20129-2  (softcover)
    1. Church group work with youth—Planning.   I. Anderson, Kim, 1965–     .  II. Title.
BV4447.M815   1997
259'.23'0684—dc21                                                                                    97–34170
                                                                                                         CIP

---

*Interior design by Sue Vandenberg Koppenol*

*Printed in the United States of America*

---

99 00 01 02 03 04 /❖ DC/ 10 9 8 7 6 5

*Dedicated to the members of the*
*Student Impact Programming Team,*
*who have committed their time, talents, and treasures*
*to the church and its cause of reaching high school students*
*for Jesus Christ, and whose reward lies on the other side.*

# Contents

# Foreword

There are those who say that very few people make a decision to follow Jesus Christ as a direct result of attending a program. They contend that true life change happens only as a result of relationships, one-on-one or in a small group. I believe these statements are true, yet they are not complete. They do not tell the whole story. Most adults and students come to faith and mature as believers through an interweaving, complex series of events, relationships, and processes. The journey to God's Kingdom involves significant influences of many dimensions along the path. All of our stories are fascinating when we relate how our Creator called us to become His followers. But while every story is different, some common threads emerge.

For many of us, among the significant contributors to life transformation have been a youth group event, church service, or Christian concert that moved our hearts, penetrated our souls, and challenged our minds. The use of the arts and creative, relevant biblical teaching are powerful tools God uses. I have seen evidence of such power ever since I was a part of a dynamic high school youth group in the 1970s. There I saw fellow students gradually come to a point of surrendering their entire futures to God after consistent participation in weekly outreach events. These programs were designed especially to communicate to nonchurched students. The music, multimedia, drama, message, and even the stage design were all planned with a specific audience in mind. We were well-led and well-taught. Most important, God was at work in the lives of a small group of believing students. In three short years my life was transformed, and the lives of many of my friends who were far from God were revolutionized as well.

I challenge you to read this book with a sense of urgency. Programs do matter. They are useless without relationships, leadership, prayer, and all the other vital aspects of biblical communities. But when we surrender our artistic and teaching gifts to the God who assigned them, when we lovingly build teams and shepherd our flocks, when we painstakingly brainstorm and prepare creative and powerful material, amazing things can happen! The Holy Spirit touches lives in ways we may never fully know about until we celebrate in heaven. Your labor will not be in vain (1 Cor. 15:58), and you will possess a deep sense of fulfillment from stewarding your gifts and ministry with the very best you could bring.

These pages contain extremely practical and proven suggestions from a godly leader I deeply respect. It is my hope that you will ask our Lord to give you wisdom to discern how you need to apply and adapt these principles to your unique ministry. But my even stronger hope is that someday a student who does not yet know Jesus Christ will experience transformation over time partly because he or she met God through moments in your programs and teaching times. What we do really does matter. In fact, it can count for all eternity.

Nancy Beach
Director of Programming
Willow Creek Community Church

# Acknowledgments

This book started as a dream that was formed from my life's journey but was completed by the hearts, minds, and hands of others:

Kim Anderson and Jane Vogel, who put more than their minds into this project; they gave their hearts. Your encouragement inspired me.

Bill Hybels and Nancy Beach, who pioneered many of the thoughts and values in this book. Your spiritual leadership has changed my life.

The Student Impact staff, who, over the past eight years, have lived out the value of team. I have learned from all of you.

Bo Boshers, who followed God's call on his life to build a vision for the church into high school students. Your vision is in these pages.

Gloria, Brandon, Tiffany, and Trevor Boshers, who took me in as one of their own. I will always love your family.

My mom, who has modeled for me what it really means to have faith in Christ. You are my hero.

Trevor and Tisha, my brother and sister, who have always been there for me, no matter what the cost. I love just being with you.

Lauren, Jacqlynn, and Hailee, who are God's daily instruments for shaping my soul and showing me snapshots of our Father. I am honored to be your dad.

Tricia, my wife, who has always been by my side and has truly become my best friend. I couldn't have written a word of this without you.

And my Heavenly Father, who loves me just the way I am.

# Introduction

## Programming:
## Painting an Image of God

Imagine it's Friday afternoon and you're sitting in your office. Once again it has been a very busy week. But now the meetings and appointments are finally over, and at last you have a chance to think about Sunday. Your message is close to be being done, but you feel that something's missing—in fact, it's been missing for a while now. Every Sunday you teach your students about Jesus Christ, but you always leave with a sense that they didn't hear it the way you intended. You feel like a professor with a bored classroom of students.

This Sunday, you determine, is going to be different. You begin to brainstorm some creative ideas that will make this message one they will never forget. You think up a great idea for a video and a song. You envision a drama that will help the message come alive for students in a powerful new way. You pull together a great plan for the session. But then reality hits—Sunday is only two days away. You can't afford to rent anything, everybody is busy this weekend, and you are out of time. It would take a modern-day miracle to pull off just one of your ideas.

Can you remember the last time you experienced a similar situation? Those of us involved in the weekly schedules of ministry face this kind of tension each week. We want so badly to teach God's Word effectively and make a difference in students' lives, but we also realize the limitations of time, money, volunteers, and resources that put a damper on our ideas and efforts. So how do you consistently create programs that glorify God and spiritually energize those listening? I believe it boils down to a process.

Author Stephen Covey states: "The greatest value of the process is not what it does to your schedule, but what it does to your head. As you begin to think more in terms of importance, you begin to see time differently. You become empowered to put first things first in your life in a significant way."[1] Every one of us can experience this empowering feeling by simply developing a purposeful process. We need an approach to our weekly responsibilities that will not only bring ideas to life but, more important, will allow God's message to penetrate the hearts of the youth of today. This process is called *programming*.

Many people respond to the idea of programming in one of two ways. Some oppose it because they see it as a marketing strategy or a way to "wow" people to Christ with bright lights, loud music, and a watered-down message. Others think that programming is all there is in ministry because they see it as the "answer" to how to draw in more students. They believe if they can put up lights, turn up the sound, and give a motivational message, people will come and stay. Both of these viewpoints are far from what programming is and can be.

*The American Heritage Dictionary* defines *programming* as "the designing, scheduling, or planning of a program."[2] Notice that there is no mention of videos, lights, or music (although any of these might be part of your program at one time or another). Programming in ministry is simply a purposeful process that will assist in communicating the Word of God. It is about carefully thinking through each opportunity to share God's Word and determining which elements to use and when.

It is our responsibility to take advantage of every chance we have to speak about God. Paul spoke about that responsibility in Colossians 4:2–4: "Devote yourselves to prayer, being watchful and thankful. And pray for us, too, that God may open a door for our message, so that we may proclaim the mystery of Christ, for which I am in chains. Pray that I may proclaim it clearly, as I should." We need to be praying and watching for any opportunity to share the mystery of Jesus Christ through our best efforts and a clear presentation.

Whether attendance is high or low, budgets big or nonexistent, God has given each of us a canvas of time to paint a picture of who He is. We are like artists who sit in front of a blank canvas, not exactly sure how the picture is going to look in the end. Somehow, the artist visualizes an image and begins to gather paint and brushes and all the tools necessary to bring the image to life on the canvas.

Maybe you can relate to that feeling of staring at a blank canvas. Perhaps you know what picture you want to see at the end, but are unsure how to go about painting it. Programming involves sorting and pulling together the arts—the creative elements like video, drama, dance, music, graphics, stage designs, props, speaking, etc.—into an order that will effectively communicate to the hearts of students.

I believe we need to go to this blank canvas with no pressure to fill slots with bands, music, lights, or videos. Rather, we should quiet ourselves and ask, "What is the Holy Spirit directing us to communicate to this particular audience? What is the image He wants us to paint, and how can we best do that with the arts available to us today?" We begin to develop a process that will cause us to become more responsible with the opportunity we have.

Because God is the Master Artist and has a unique plan for the blank canvas in your ministry, I am unable to tell you how you should paint your canvas. Instead, in this book I will share an eleven-step process, divided into four phases, you can use to transfer the image God wants *you* to paint for your ministry onto your canvas.

The four phases in this book contain synergistic steps of development that are like gears, moving and functioning together simultaneously. These gears can be adjusted, rearranged, and tweaked to fit your ministry or personal needs. Prayer is the oil that will remove any friction or sticking points in the gears, and needs to be a nonnegotiable part of your program development process.

A word of caution: As Christians, we are called to be image-bearers of Christ. We must regularly ask ourselves, "Am I becoming more like Christ each day?" Before we can paint an image of God publicly, we must take a close look at the image we are painting privately. As it was modeled by Jesus Christ and other godly men and women in Scripture, our private spiritual life must be in order before we begin any public ministry. Programming must begin with a submitted, humble heart and moldable spirit. Each of us must be willing to do the hard work of character building in order to become more like Christ.

Take a moment to evaluate your heart before reading on. As you pray, thank God for allowing you to serve in ministry and ask Him for the Holy Spirit's direction as you seek to improve your programs. My prayer is that God would touch your heart and mind so that you are ready and able to take steps in learning how to paint an image of Him.

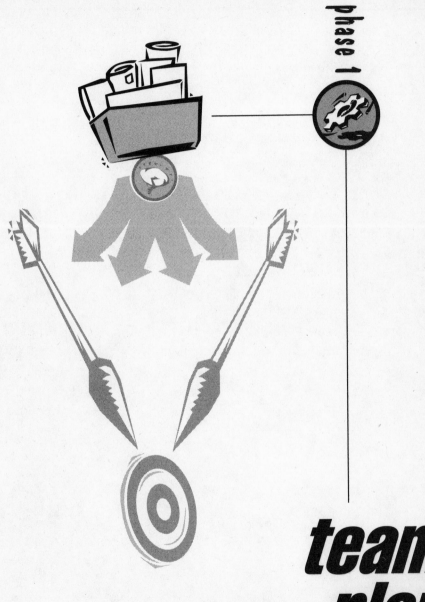

*team*
*plan*
*purpose*

# Step

# team

## We are stronger when we work together

I t was a radical plan that seemed ridiculous at the time. A plan that would challenge every mind and heart, educated or not, young or old, for the rest of time. It did away with the spiritual ladder-climbing that had prevailed for so many years. The plan needed people, but required no applications, no interviews, and no educational certificates. In fact, the plan received much resistance for one simple reason: it was available to anyone who would believe, regardless of race, political or financial status, gender, or education. The plan is still working today. We call it the church.

The church started with an unlikely group of 120 people who followed Jesus and committed every part of their lives to building His church. Little did this group realize that they were laying the foundation for a divine organism that would last for eternity.

The beauty of God's plan, the church, isn't just brick and mortar, pews, and steeples. His church is made with people. He built within each of us a basic need for relationships, a need to be connected with others. Jesus knew that we could be stronger and more effective together than apart, so He shattered the existing religious isolation and individualism and created a movement involving people being together. It's no mistake that the most important and powerful plan for humankind has "team" as its core value.

The first step in the programming process is to build a team. We, as leaders, need a team of people who can work together to accomplish God's purpose of redeeming lost students. I believe that we will be held accountable not only for the work God has called us to, but also for how we do that work: together.

## What Is a Team?

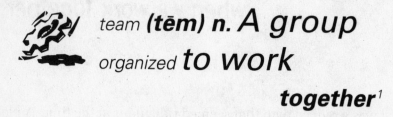

team *(tēm) n.* A group organized to work together[1]

Teams exist for several different purposes. In the athletic arena a team's purpose is to win. In the business arena a team's purpose is to profit. In the military arena a team's purpose is to conquer. John F. Kennedy set a goal to place a man on the moon by 1970, and a team was developed to make that goal become a reality. And who can forget the American hockey team that overcame the odds to beat the Soviet team and win the gold medal in the 1980 Winter Olympics? Teams with a purpose can accomplish great things. Envision what you can accomplish with a team whose purpose it is to paint an image of God!

Business experts Jon Katzenbach and Douglas Smith define a team as "a small number of people with complementary skills who are committed to a common purpose, performance goals, and approach for which they hold themselves mutually accountable."[2] I wonder how many of us have actually experienced that definition. Is the purpose of your ministry clear and so compelling that your team is committed to doing everything they can in order to accomplish it? My best team experiences have been when every person on the team shared a common purpose that drove every minute of our lives. On those teams we had no titles, no offices, no paychecks, no public recognition, no marked territory, only a "hands in the middle" and "I'll give it my all and my best" kind of attitude.

I was a part of that kind of team as a nineteen-year-old in southern California. I remember what our small team looked like as we met in a rented private high school in Burbank. We were an unlikely group of young sinners who had no credentials or official training, only a passion to give the best we had to God and serve Him. There wasn't much we wouldn't do to accomplish our purpose. We met for our staff meetings, eager to share how God was working and to decide what we needed to do next. What was especially gratifying was that we all won together; each team member wanted the others to succeed, and we never did anything alone. We did whatever it took to see our ministry grow in the community and in our own lives. We held each other accountable and became a spiritually connected group that changed the community. We were united by a common and compelling purpose, each of us contributing to the team in a special way.

On God's team, each member has a unique place and a God-given role to play. From 1 Corinthians 12 we learn that each of us has been given a spiritual gift, a divine enablement to contribute to the body. First Corinthians 12:27 says, "Now you are the body of Christ, and each one of you is a part of it." Programming teams are microcosms of the body of Christ. As you build a programming team, help others identify their unique gifts and place them according to those strengths. Your goal should be to work together as a team and value each gift so that the body of Christ can function as He intended. Amazing things will happen once every believer realizes the role he or she is to play on the team!

That first team experience helped me identify my spiritual gifts. I was encouraged to use my gift of leadership and develop it as best I could. The team placed me in a role that fit my maturity level and strength, and I have continued to grow and use that gift today.

The programming team of which I am currently a part is made up of approximately fifty people who use their spiritual gifts and invest their resources, time, and energy to make God's truths come alive to high school students. My role as Program Director is to lead the programming team and provide direction, leadership, encouragement, shepherding, and vision-casting to the group. Within the larger team are four smaller, specialized teams: drama, production (lights, sound, and stage), music (band and vocalists), and video. It would be virtually impossible (and overwhelming!) for me to try to lead all fifty of these people, so each of these teams is managed and led by a director.

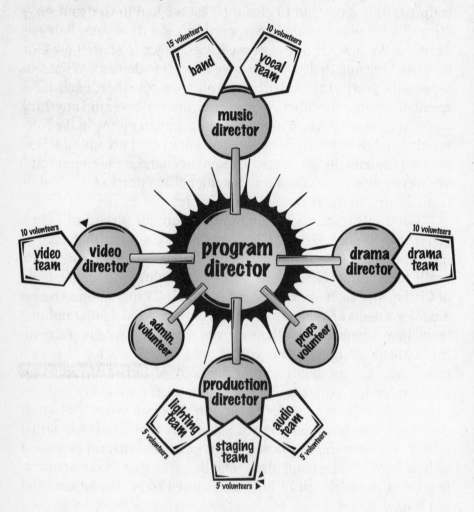

Each team is crucial to our program's effectiveness; we work together and strive to maintain our interconnectedness. On the night of a program, we pray for one another, work with each other, and cheer each other on. The video team knows that the members of the drama team have spent time rehearsing and are prepared. The band knows beforehand that they play a song right after the drama, so they are excited to take the baton. The production team has their cues for sound and lighting all set and are anticipating each element. We all count on each other to do our parts in painting an image of God for our audience.

While every person has a different role, no person is more important than the other. Stephen Covey, founder and chairman of the Covey Leadership Center, would call this kind of teamwork *synergy*. "Synergy results from valuing differences by bringing different perspectives together in the spirit of mutual respect."[3] Covey may call it synergy; God calls it the church.

Every week, our team realizes that we do together what we could never do alone. "Humility comes as we realize that 'no man is an island,' that no one individual has all the talents, all the ideas, all the capacity to perform the functions of the whole. Vital to quality of life is the ability to work together, learn from each other, and help each other grow."[4] Thank God that He gave us the church!

## Why Build a Team?

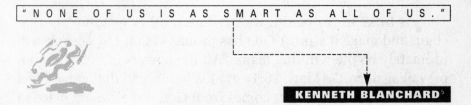

"NONE OF US IS AS SMART AS ALL OF US."

KENNETH BLANCHARD[5]

Our church campus has a large pond out front where many geese have taken up residence. Geese are fascinating birds. I have learned that an incredible interdependence exists among geese. For example, when it's time to migrate, geese fly in a "V" formation. As each bird flaps its wings, an uplift is created for the bird behind. Flying this way adds seventy-one percent greater flying range than if each bird flew alone.[6] If a goose falls out of formation, it rapidly feels the drag and resistance of trying to fly alone. A smart goose quickly rejoins the formation in order to take advantage of the lifting power of the bird in front.

Like a goose who falls out of formation, those who try to do ministry all alone are soon exhausted. By yourself, you won't last very long or get very far. When you expend your energy to complete ministry projects and goals alone, you buy into the "old plan" of individualism. You will only frustrate yourself, your family, your friends, and—in the end—the listeners, who will not receive the best. The bottom line is that you will "burn out"—and most likely burn out those listening to you.

It is imperative to realize that the vehicle God designed for us to create and develop these programs is the church—the body of Christ. Dietrich Bonhoeffer, in his book *Life Together*, states:

> In a Christian community everything depends upon whether each individual is an indispensable link in a chain. Only when even the smallest link is securely interlocked is the chain unbreakable. A community which allows unemployed members to exist within it will perish because of them. It will be well, therefore, if every member receives a definite task to perform for the community, that he may know in hours of doubt that he, too, is not useless and unusable. Every Christian community must realize that not only do the weak need the strong, but also that the strong cannot exist without the weak. The elimination of the weak is the death of fellowship.[7]

As links in the chain, we need each other to complete that chain and make it strong. God has promised that His church will ultimately be the winning team: "All the powers of hell shall not prevail against it" (Matt. 16:18 TLB).When I read that verse I feel a spiritual confidence that comes from God. I realize my place in the big picture and understand my responsibility to "link" together all those with the common purpose to create programs that will change lives.

With all the benefits of working as a team, why have so many believers not caught on to this heavenly plan? Part of the problem is rooted in the fact that "we grow up under a regimen that measures (academic grades), rewards (allowances), and punishes (trips to the principal's office) individual—not collective—performance. Whenever we want to 'get something done,' our first thought is that of holding an individual responsible."[8] Our culture bombards us daily with individualistic messages like "You are the most important"; "Make yourself look good"; "Prove yourself"; "Do it yourself"; "Promote yourself." It shouldn't come as a surprise that some of us try to "do ministry" on our own. We think we can do it all ourselves, or we crave some individual recognition. But in doing so, we miss out on the opportunity to minister as a team, a part of the body. When we attempt to do programming without a team, we court the danger of our ministry becoming ours and not God's.

The sad fact for many of us is that we have to keep relearning the value of team. Sometimes it's a hard and lonely lesson. In a one-year season at Student Impact, we offer approximately one hundred scheduled programs. At some point each year, I find myself doing ministry alone because I believe the lie: "I have to do this right. I can't trust anyone else, so I must do it myself." I regularly need to relearn that when God brings a group of people together for a specific purpose, each member's contribution is valuable. In the end, it becomes better together than anything I would have done alone.

This truth always becomes evident when our team plans and produces our camp programs. Each year our ministry offers a winter weekend retreat and a week-long summer camp, both of which are held off-site and never disappoint us in the way of challenges. Meeting rooms that are too small or a facility with no electricity introduces us to adversity and forces our group to become a team. We used to hold our summer camp at a place with no electricity or running water. Imagine that brainstorming session! The limitations forced us, in a positive way, to work together and be innovative, different, creative, and visionary in planning programs.

No matter what obstacle has been before us, our team has rallied together and come to camp with hands outstretched to serve. To me, it's a mental snapshot of why God created the church and how He intended it to function.

## How Do You Build a Team?

 *"Great leaders often inspire their followers to high levels of achievement by showing them how their work contributes to worthwhile ends. It is an emotional appeal to some of the most fundamental of human needs—the need to be important, to make a difference, to feel useful, to be a part of a successful and worthwhile enterprise."*

WARREN BENNIS AND BURT NANUS[9]

Imagine observing a program where the vocalist communicated a song that touched your soul, the drama actor played a realistic role that felt like you, the media powerfully presented truthful imagery that was captivating, the teacher taught God's Word with boldness, and the sound and lights accented each element just right. It's exciting to be a part of a program like this, where the right person is positioned in the right place based on spiritual gifts. It's amazing to see God work through gifted people who are put in a position to use those gifts.

Building a team like this takes time and requires that you carefully and prayerfully select people according to their gifts, spiritual maturity, skills and experience, and time availability. Trying to just fill holes with warm bodies will lead to frustration and ineffective team-building.

When Dale Carnegie was asked his secret for developing leaders within his organization, he replied, "Men are developed the same way gold is mined. Several tons of dirt must be moved to get an ounce of gold. But you don't go into the mine looking for dirt," he added. "You go in looking for the gold."[10] We, too, should look for the gold in people and see their value and potential.

Each programming team will have its own unique combination of personalities, but certain spiritual gifts should be represented on every team. First, it's important to have people with the gift of creative communication—people who are gifted in the arts, like music, visual art, and drama. People with this gift will have a very public ministry and most likely end up being in front of an audience. Make the effort to get to know each person's heart and motivation for service. Are they looking to please their own egos or to serve God? Artists can sometimes be tempted to glorify themselves rather than God, so be wise in the selection process.

Second, you need to find at least one innovative, creative thinker who doesn't need to go to an art museum to get creative ideas; he or she can see creativity in a hardware store. This person will be able to prime the idea pump for the team. Look for people in your church or relational circle who always seems to say "I've got a great idea" or "What if . . . ?" You can usually identify this type of creative person over time by listening to how he or she dreams or gets excited about something.

Third, your team needs people with leadership gifts. The stakes are too high and the task too difficult without leadership. Leaders can lead specialized programming teams, like music, drama, video, lights, or sound production, and are able to both lead people and complete the tasks. Look for people who can take a project and carry it out to completion without "killing" those people under their direction in the process. You would be wise to wait until the right leaders are in place, or you, like Moses in Exodus 18, will wear yourself out.

The fourth spiritual gift that will breathe life into your team is the gift of helps. People with this gift are "can do" people who love to serve behind the scenes. Their contribution to the team is vital. They can assist in a variety of ways, from preprogram set-up to sorting out copies of a cue sheet. People whose hearts beat fast at the thought of doing behind-the-scenes jobs that will serve the team are indeed treasures. Look for those who love to help or seem willing to do anything.

And fifth, include as many people with the gift of shepherding as possible. The shepherds of the team will make sure that people are always more important than programs and that the programming process honors those involved. Listen to how Phillip Keller describes a shepherd:

> Whenever the shepherd comes to the fold it is for the benefit of the sheep. Unlike the rustlers or predators who come to raid or rob the livestock within, he always comes with beneficial intentions. The sheep do not fear him. They do not flee in panic or rush about in bewildered confusion, trampling and maiming each other in blind excitement.[11]

You can identify a shepherd by looking for those people who are always encouraging others, showing care and concern for people, or taking the time to listen as people talk.

Obviously, God uses many gifts to accomplish His purposes. You need to pray and trust that He will bring to and place the right people on your team. If you find yourself doing programs and events all alone, stop! Go and get connected with other believers and begin building a team. Find that common purpose. Identify believers who will help you paint an image of God to the students in your ministry. Pray for God to bring those people who share your vision and mission. And remember that this can take more time than you projected, so be patient.

*try this . . .*

- Define on paper what you and the ministry you are leading are all about. Where would you like to take the ministry? Then take every opportunity you can to share that vision with those around you. You will be surprised how many people resonate with your vision.
- You may already have a team of people serving with you. Identify the strengths, weaknesses, and spiritual gifts of each person. Based on your findings, are they serving in the right place on your team or do you need to make some adjustments? What spiritual gifts are missing from your team? Let each person know how his or her gift fits uniquely into the team.
- If you don't already have one scheduled, begin holding weekly programming staff team meetings to rally and teach the staff about teams. This can eventually become a great time to build a sense of community.
- Ask your pastor if he would allow the high school ministry a chance to program a weekend church service. Don't just sing; do the whole service! Your congregation will catch a glimpse of the high school ministry and generational bridges can be built. And an added benefit to your programming team is that new programming volunteers may surface after observing the service.
- Ask your pastor to teach on the topic of spiritual gifts in order to help the members of your church discover their spiritual gifts. At the end of his message or series, hold a ministry fair. Invite a representative from every ministry in your church to staff a booth and explain the ministry opportunities available in his or her particular ministry. Prepare each booth with written information (a creative flyer or brochure) describing the serving opportunities available on that team. You could even plug in a monitor by each booth and show a video of a recent program. You may find several people interested in joining your programming team.

- On a piece of paper, describe your ideal programming team, with ministry descriptions for various service opportunities. Be sure to include a specific description of the time commitment, spiritual gifts, and experience (if any) needed. Doing this will prepare you to see what you need and strategically place volunteers appropriately on your team.
- Investigate local colleges in your area for potential volunteers. Start with video, theater, drama, and dance classes. Look for the best, but allow God to pull the right team together. Remember: they may not look like the most ideal bunch!

**Caution:** Never compromise your programs by putting a person on a team who is talented in an area but who lacks a committed, servant's heart or is motivated by a performance mind-set. Such a person will only bring the team down. Each team member must be a committed believer of integrity. This may mean that you involve high school students who are not as developed in their gifts, but who are sold out on your ministry's vision and who love the Lord.

**more resources**

Blanchard, Kenneth. *The One Minute Manager Builds High Performing Teams.* New York: William Morrow and Company, Inc., 1990.

Bonhoeffer, Dietrich. *Life Together.* San Francisco: Harper San Francisco, 1954.

Boshers, Bo. *Student Ministry for the 21st Century.* Grand Rapids: Zondervan, 1997.

Covey, Stephen R., Roger A. Merrill, and Rebecca R. Merrill. *First Things First.* New York: Simon & Schuster, 1994.

Katzenbach, Jon R., and Douglas K. Smith. *The Wisdom of Teams.* New York: Harper Business, 1993.

Maxwell, John C. *Developing the Leaders Around You.* Nashville: Thomas Nelson, 1995.

Ogden, Greg. *The New Reformation.* Grand Rapids: Zondervan, 1990.

Shula, Don and Ken Blanchard. *Everyone's a Coach.* Grand Rapids: Zondervan, 1995.

# Step 2

# *plan*

## What does the future look like?

It probably was or will be the biggest day of your life. Every minute is accounted for. Every element of the day is carefully selected. Invitations, caterers, decorations, and flowers must be just right. You choose the location and every note of music, not to entertain, but to communicate something meaningful. Each person's placement, steps, and words are thoughtfully organized. Rehearsing for this sixty-minute event is so important that you practice it a day before and celebrate it with a big dinner. It's the one day where everything is important and nothing is too much to ask in order to make it right: your wedding day.

Whether your wedding was (or will be) small and simple or large and detailed, you'd probably agree that a lot of planning and preparation was necessary to make the day special. But to you and your soon-to-be spouse, it was a worthwhile investment of time and energy because it was important to you both.

We plan for those events, programs, and activities that are of value to us. To me, sharing the love of Christ with high school students is an incredible privilege, and one I take seriously. Yet I am often convicted by my lack of prayerful planning for programs that have eternal stakes. It's a continual challenge to value planning from eternity's perspective.

How much time and energy do you spend planning the program schedule for your ministry season? In this chapter, we'll learn about step two in the programming process: plan. Later in the book, we'll take a closer look at how to use the arts and develop specific program events. For now, let's explore the critical role planning plays in developing the flow of a ministry year.

## What Is Planning?

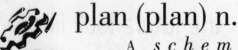 plan (plan) n.
A *s c h e m e ,    p r o g r a m ,*
or *m e t h o d* worked out beforehand for the
*a c c o m p l i s h m e n t* of an
*o b j e c t i v e*[1]

Planning in programming involves intentionally and proactively looking at the ministry calendar and deciding which programs should be developed and when they will take place. Or, as Robert M. Donnelly somewhat sardonically comments, "Planning is deciding why you are going to do something before you do it, rather than the easier way of doing something and then trying to figure out why you did it."[2]

I have found it helpful to sit down with our team before the ministry season begins, while the calendar is still blank, and schedule a whole ministry season. Obviously, we do not plan each program and event in detail, but we look closely at the calendar and ask:

- When and how long will each topical series last?
- Which holidays and school breaks do we need to plan around?
- When during the year is momentum usually high, and when is it low?
- What do we want to accomplish by the end of the ministry season? Which events can best help us accomplish this?

Answering these questions allows us to plan the ministry year most effectively. We also solicit input from other sources. Someone might bring some information about school holidays, vacations, and game schedules from various high schools. Our parents' team offers suggestions that assist our planning efforts, like ideas for specific events, or the best time of year, based on family vacations, to offer certain programs. Inside Out, a board of students representing each of the high schools in our ministry, meets monthly, and we value the insights and opinions they share with us. We also work closely with other ministries at our church to determine when each ministry is requesting to use the church facility. The more we know in advance, the more effective are our "big picture" planning efforts.

## Why Plan?

> 66 We must pay the price of investing careful planning and attention to detail. Advertisers spend countless hours calculating what strategies to use to persuade us to purchase their product. Surely, as stewards of the eternal truths of salvation and hope, we can commit ourselves to a process of devoted planning. 99
>
> **nancy beach**[3]

My wife, Tricia, and I take turns planning our date nights on the weekends. One weekend not too long ago it was my turn to create the evening plan. I had great intentions that week to plan a special date, but my schedule got out of balance and I didn't plan a single minute of it. In fact, it was only as I drove home from the church that Friday that I came up with a spontaneous plan that offered excitement and adventure. Or so I thought.

When I arrived home, I came in the door all smiles and told Tricia to get ready for our date night. Tricia asked me what to wear. I hadn't thought through the whole clothing deal so I gave the safe answer: "Casual, but kind of nice."

At that point, I think Tricia started to smell my deception. We jumped into the car and I began to drive to the restaurant I had in mind. "No reservations? It will be an hour wait," the hostess said. My well-thought-out evening didn't get any better from that point on. As I tried to explain to Tricia why I hadn't planned the evening in advance, I learned a big lesson. Tricia didn't mind the spontaneity or the one-hour wait. She was upset that I didn't care enough to plan.

People can tell how much you value something or someone by the planning effort you put into it. Planning a date with Tricia didn't mean every minute had to be mapped out. But to communicate value to her, I should have thought ahead and prepared. This date needed to cost me something—not necessarily money, but my time and my heart.

In the same way, planning communicates value to those to whom we minister. Do your students know you value them? When was the last time you carved out an extended period of time and devoted it to preparing for the future of your ministry? Students will sense a lack of value if your planning efforts are minimal. They will not be fooled.

Not only does planning communicate value, it also gives a long-term rather than a short-term view. Management expert Peter Drucker argues that one of the reasons the Japanese have been so successful in business is that "they start out by saying, Where should we be ten years hence? And we start by saying, What should be the bottom line for the quarter?" [4]

I think sometimes those of us in church work consider planning a waste of time. We take Matthew 6:34, "Therefore do not worry about tomorrow, for tomorrow will worry about itself. Each day has enough trouble of its own," as an excuse to avoid looking to the future. But Dr. Eugene Habecker, President of the American Bible Society, argues that "planning ought to be seen as a legitimate function of biblical stewardship. As followers of Christ, we believe that we have a stewardship responsibility for all the resources that God has given to us. In brief, we believe we cannot practice good stewardship unless our planning helps us make the most of our resources." [5]

Planning allows you to be a good steward of the resources God has entrusted to your ministry by providing overall direction and purpose to your ministry. A common pitfall we can fall into is filling up the calendar with last-minute activities and wasting resources on activities that are not purposeful. Students then bounce from one activity or event to the next without really knowing why or where the ministry is headed. They become program-driven. Planning helps you fulfill your ministry's objectives throughout the year while allowing you to decide which activities and programs are purposeful and worth doing. You can then be a wise steward with your time, your volunteers, and your finances.

## How Do You Plan?

**"THE ESSENCE OF GOOD PLANNING IS ASKING**

*'why?'*

AND

*'then what?'*

UNTIL WHAT HAS TO BE DONE TO GET FROM
WHERE YOU ARE TO WHERE YOU WANT TO BE BECOMES

*crystal clear."*

**ROBERT M. DONNELLY**[6]

Planning in programming involves no magic formula or set standards. God leads each ministry in different ways. It is our responsibility to listen closely to those leadings and then act accordingly. While it will be necessary for you to customize your planning process based on God's leadings, your ministry's vision and mission, and the culture unique to your particular ministry, I would like to offer three principles I use in our ministry's planning process: "get away often"; "always think ahead"; and "build momentum."

"Getting away often" means just what it says—get away! You and your team need to find a place with few distractions for a team planning meeting or retreat. Meeting in the office, on the church campus, or even at home often opens the door to interruptions and frustration. You need to "unplug" from the schedule and clear your heart, mind, and soul so that you make decisions from quietness rather than from busyness.

It's also important to get away by yourself before planning. I am always working on this discipline in my own life: spending some solitude time with God. I often find a small, quiet coffee shop and journal in order to prepare my heart before planning.

The second principle I use in the planning process is "always think ahead." In ministry, I believe one of Satan's greatest tools is busyness. Too often, I have caught myself making quick and rushed choices about big events. This last-minute thinking usually ends up hurting our program instead of helping it. Do you find yourself making irrational decisions because you are too busy to slow down and think? What mistakes could you prevent by taking the time to think through a decision? Do you value the ministry and your students enough to carve out time to plan? When you begin to think this way, you can identify more easily the areas that may need attention, like you or your team members' pace of life; the giftedness and health of the volunteers involved in your programs; or scheduling conflicts with upcoming holidays or breaks, to name a few. You will then have enough time to address any problems and avoid program disasters.

The third principle I use in planning is to "build momentum." Look for opportunities to build on what happened in previous program events. One of the best ways to build momentum is to block off time for a series of programs on the same topic. For instance, if you run a program on Wednesday evenings and you can schedule six Wednesday nights in a row, use those six successive weeks to develop a theme. We have learned that a series of three weeks or less is not effective for building momentum. As you plan, fit in as many series blocks as your calendar and students' pace of life will permit.

*try this . . .*

Arrange an extended meeting or retreat two to four times a year with your staff or team of volunteers to discuss the ministry's values and schedule and to plan for the next season. Taking the time to think, evaluate, and agree on a course of action as a team will lead to planning with purpose.

Try planning with a long-term view. Start by looking one year down the road and then, at a different planning session, five years down the road.

Here are some questions to generate good discussions and dreams at your retreats:

- What events do we need to schedule that will help achieve our vision?
- What will we accomplish in one year with our current schedule?
- What is missing from our current schedule? What needs to improve?
- What life change could happen in our students' lives this year?
- What areas of programming are we doing well? What can we celebrate?
- What year/month/week schedule are we capable of handling with the current team?
- How will our lives be changed with a potential new schedule? Will life be manageable?
- How many series blocks can we fit into the schedule?
- What scheduled events are unnecessary and need to be changed or eliminated?
- What changes can we make now that will pay off later?
- When is the best time for our audience to attend programs or events?
- Who are the players necessary for this plan? Are they already on the team or do we need to build our team further?
- What training is needed to make this plan successful?
- How can we best serve together as a team?

After you work through some or all of these questions, put a dry-erase calendar (year-at-a-glance) on the wall. Now you are ready to begin putting together the skeleton schedule for the year. Remember, the object isn't to just fill up your calendar with activities, but to think through each and every date you mark on the calendar.

Once you have decided on a program and penciled it onto the calendar, schedule a weekly meeting with your team to develop these programs in detail. You will read more about how to do this in chapter 10.

**more resources**

Biehl, Bobb. *Increasing Your Leadership Confidence*. Sisters, Ore.: Questar, 1989.

Borthwick, Paul. *Organizing Your Youth Ministry*. Grand Rapids: Zondervan, 1988.

Donnelly, Robert M. *Guidebook to Planning*. New York: Van Nostrand Reinhold Company, 1984.

Drucker, Peter F. *Managing the Non-Profit Organization*. New York: Harper Collins, 1990.

MacDonald, Gordon. *Ordering Your Private World*. Nashville: Oliver-Nelson, 1984.

# Step 3

# *purpose*

## Don't purposely do everything, but do everything with purpose

think about your last ministry program. How did it go? What did you do? More important, why did you do it? I hope you were able to clearly answer the question "why." In the last chapter we discussed the role of "big picture" planning and looking closely at your ministry calendar. Once you have planned and chosen program dates, you and your team are now ready to focus on and determine each program's specific purpose. Purpose-driven ministry changes lives. I'd like to share with you how it changed mine.

### The Power of Purpose-Driven Ministry

In 1982 I was a senior at a Christian high school in southern California. At that point in my Christian life, I had begun asking myself some serious questions: "Is this all there is to Christianity? Do I still want to be part of it?" I had grown up in a church with a great facility. The medium-sized youth group to which I belonged offered a lot of fun activities and retreats, and the band was pretty cool. But each time I went, I knew something was missing; I just couldn't figure out what.

I finally decided I had had enough of playing the church game, so I started searching for something else to help me deal with life and its struggles. I traveled down some other roads of which I'm not proud, but they only left me more empty.

That year, my high school hired a new football coach named Bo. We seniors disliked him immediately and made it clear that he wasn't going to get anything from us until he earned our trust. Throughout the season, however, I couldn't help but notice something very different about this coach's lifestyle. He didn't play the "Christian game." I kept a close eye on him and tried to figure out what made him tick.

It was close to the end of our season when Bo invited me to a student Bible study he led called "Come and Enjoy." It's a wonder that I ever attended an event with such a bad name! I couldn't believe he invited me, an arrogant senior who didn't trust him! But because he had intrigued me with his life, I couldn't refuse.

I remember my first visit to the group like it was yesterday. When I showed up, the twenty to thirty students present were my age. They were friendly, and I noticed that they had the same mysterious way about them as Bo.

The room in which we met was very plain and contained no youth posters or special banners. There were no fancy lights and no band. It was just a classroom with school chairs and a chalkboard. As I sat down, I wondered what would happen. Without all the "extras" like lights and a band, I thought it was bound to be worse than my church youth group. To my surprise, Bo taught from the Bible like no one else I had ever heard. I understood what he was saying, and it felt like he was talking only to me.

Toward the end of his message, Bo decided to challenge the group by asking us to imagine that we had all possible resources like money and materials available to us, and that any idea we conceived could become a reality. With that thought in mind, he gave us one guideline (to do it together) and one purpose (to build the greatest rollercoaster ride ever known to man).

I wondered what this was all about. It felt a little awkward, but the next few minutes were about to change my life forever. I watched and listened as several students raised their hands and gave suggestions with excitement and energy, as if this rollercoaster were a real thing. For the first time, I witnessed students becoming an active part of something. Part way through the discussion, I decided to become a participant instead of just an observer, and that is when I first experienced contributing to something that was bigger than myself.

Finally, Bo put down his Bible, turned to us and said, "We are God's chosen people, His children, and He has already given us all the resources that we need. He promises always to be there for us so that we can accomplish one purpose: to build a student ministry that has never been built before. It will be a place where lost high school students can come and be saved!"

At that moment, God touched my soul with His purpose. I not only wanted to help build that ride, I jumped on it with both hands in the air. For the first time, the void in my life was filled with a purpose, God's purpose: to build a place where my friends could come and learn about Him. From that day on, I started to understand what it meant to be a part of the body of Christ, a part of His team, a part of a ministry that wouldn't offer activities and programs just to occupy time, but that had a clear purpose in mind. I learned that day that lights, bands, and, "cool" activities were not the secret to a vibrant student ministry, Jesus Christ was. The picture of His purpose was painted to me more clearly than ever before. No band, drama, stage, lights, or decibel level would have ever done that.

## What Is Purpose?

**pur•pose (pûr′pes) n.**

*The object toward which one strives or for which something exists; an aim or a goal*[1]

One of the most attractive parts of my first ministry experience with Bo was that everything our group did had a reason, a purpose. Whenever I felt unclear about an event's or program's purpose, I would ask, "Why are we doing this?" I could always trust that I would hear "why" we did anything. As leaders, we must be prepared to answer that question for our students.

Purpose is knowing why you do the things you do. It is having a clear view of what your ministry wants to accomplish (mission), where you want it to go (vision), and how you will get there (strategy). From outreach programs to in-home Bible studies, whether large or small, every event scheduled should move toward accomplishing the ministry's vision and mission. Purpose gives you focus and a plan. Football coaching legend Woody Hayes once said, "Even the best team, without a sound plan, can't score."[2]

Purpose may seem like a simple concept, but the truth is that most of us could use a bit more focus in the midst of our busy schedules. Some of us wear multiple ministry hats, making it even more difficult to stay purpose-driven. The tyranny of the urgent is always threatening, and oftentimes we end up doing things for the wrong reasons or no reason at all. We need to stay focused on why we are doing what we are doing.

## Why Have Purpose?

"EARLIER THAN EVER BEFORE, TODAY'S SEGMENT OF TEENAGERS REALIZES THAT THEIR DECISIONS TODAY WILL SHAPE SIGNIFICANT ASPECTS OF THEIR LIFE FROM HERE ON. AND ALTHOUGH IT CONFLICTS WITH THE POPULAR NOTION OF MODERN TEENS, OUR RESEARCH HAS DISCOVERED THAT TEENS BELIEVE THAT YOU REAP WHAT YOU SOW. CONSEQUENTLY, THEY BELIEVE THAT THEY ALONE ARE RESPONSIBLE FOR WHAT THEY ULTIMATELY GET FROM LIFE AND THEY MUST, THEREFORE, STRIVE TO MAKE SOMETHING WORTHWHILE OUT OF LIFE."

GEORGE BARNA[3]

Students today, more than ever, are looking for purpose and meaning in their lives. They walk down different roads, experimenting with things they think will fill the void in their souls. Unfortunately, many of them are walking in the wrong direction:

- Every year in America, about one million young women under the age of twenty become pregnant. Every day in America, one thousand unmarried teen girls become mothers.[4] Dr. G. Keith Olsen states in his book *Counseling Teenagers* that becoming pregnant is "usually quite purposeful. Pregnancy in adolescent girls often represents an attempt to feel whole and valuable as a woman."[5]

- Of the 20.7 million students in seventh to twelfth grade nation-wide, 68 percent have drunk alcohol at least once, and 51 percent (10.6 million) have had at least one drink within the past year. Of those who drink, eight million drink weekly. By the time they reach their senior year in high school, nine out of ten teens will have experimented with alcohol, and 39 percent will get drunk at least once every two weeks.[6] The National Institute on Alcohol Abuse and Alcoholism reports that there are 3.3 million teenage alcoholics in the United States.[7]
- Six out of ten teenagers will have used illicit drugs at least once before finishing high school. In 1990, 33 percent of America's high school seniors reported using illicit drugs during the last year.[8]
- Every day in America, five hundred adolescents begin using drugs. According to a Gallup poll, "The average age at which children first try alcohol or marijuana is twelve."[9]

Whenever I read statistics like these, my heart breaks. Our youth are crying out for something to give their life meaning and are desperately looking for a way to cope with the challenges of life. Sadly, over time, students discover that sex, alcohol, and drugs are dead-end roads that will never add meaning to their lives— only take meaning from it. As a student minister, I hope you realize that you have been given a tremendous opportunity to paint an image of God to a generation searching for answers. You can point your students to the One who gives purpose and direction to life: Jesus Christ. You know the answer your students are looking for!

Programming can play a critical role in helping students learn more about Christ. Willow Creek Community Church's Programming Director, Nancy Beach, calls the part of the program preceding the message a "treasure." She believes

> For those of us who are given the responsibility to prepare the "front-door" dimension of church life, we must begin with a sense that the time in those services is not dispensable; it is not a time that we dread filling. It is not entertainment before the "really important" thing happens (the sermon). The team at Willow Creek views the thirty minutes of "programming" in our seeker services and thirty to forty-five minutes in our worship services as a treasure. We think of every single minute

as a potential treasure. What takes place in that half-hour can count for eternity. It can provide the turning point for a lost soul or healing for a wounded soldier. It does not compete with the message time; it need not devalue the role of solid biblical teaching. When the creative arts work together with well-crafted teaching—watch out! God can unleash his power in amazing ways.[10]

Every minute we have to share the love of Christ really is a treasure, like precious gold. There is no time to waste on "filler" and no reason to throw random elements together. We must be wise stewards of this gift and take every opportunity He gives us to share His love with the high school students around us.

First Peter 3:15 challenges us to "always be prepared to give an answer to everyone who asks you to give the reason for the hope that you have." Every program, meeting, or event we do should be purposeful. Eternity hangs in the balance for many of those in our audiences. They are looking for some hope to bring purpose to their lives. Surveys show that more than two-thirds of all adults who have accepted Christ made their decision to do so before the age of eighteen.[11] The time we have to impact our students for Christ is short, and the opportunity will quickly pass. Let's not waste this valuable time by offering Christian entertainment. Commit to always plan purposeful programs so that students can more clearly see an image of God.

## How Do You Establish Your Purpose?

"Every moment comes to you pregnant with divine purpose; time being so precious that God deals it out only second by second. Once it leaves your hands and your power to do with it as you please, it plunges into eternity, to remain forever what you made it."[12]
ARCHBISHOP FULTON J. SHEEN

I am privileged to be the father of three beautiful daughters: Lauren, Jacqlynn, and Hailee. Lauren is five years old and full of questions about life. She doesn't ask a lot of different questions, really, only one: "Why?" Lauren will ask me that question for everything I do or say. I have found that I will answer that question in one of two ways. I will either answer with confidence, knowing the answer, or I will give some random guess to satisfy her curiosity. That may be fine for fathering young children, but not when we are talking about programs. The first step in having a clear purpose to a program is to be able to answer the "why" question with confidence.

This step of purpose really works hand in hand with the "big picture" planning we talked about in the previous chapter. As you look at your ministry season calendar, you must evaluate whether each program has a purpose that will ultimately achieve the vision of your ministry. Anything less than that should be reconsidered and refined.

I once visited a ministry in the midwest that was steeped in decades of tradition. They had always had a program on Saturday evenings; no holiday, event, or obstacle stood in the way of their meeting time. They boasted of the fact that they had only canceled one Saturday night program, and that was because of a fire in the building. The sad part about this was that they were running their ministry off an old tradition that had lost its purpose. When I asked a few key students why they were there and what the purpose was for the evening, I got blank stares or that familiar response of "I don't know."

At Student Impact, we have decided that our purpose, or mission, is "to help nonbelieving high school students become fully devoted followers of Christ." The means to accomplish this mission flows out of our seven-step strategy, which we call full-cycle evangelism. Here's how the strategy works:

1. *Integrity friendship*: a Christian student (let's call him Tom) begins to build an integrity friendship with a non-Christian friend (let's call him Bryan).
2. *Verbal witness*: Tom shares a verbal witness (his testimony) with Bryan.
3. *Supplemental witness/seeker service*: Tom invites Bryan to a program that has been designed with a non-Christian in mind. This program, which we call Student Impact, meets most Tuesday nights and is purposely designed as a tool our Christian students use to supplement their witness to their non-Christian friends.
4. *Spiritual challenge*: Bryan sees a picture of God that touches his soul as the message-giver presents Biblical truth and offers

a spiritual challenge in the form of a question. Tom follows up by asking Bryan this question and challenges his friend to consider the claims of Christ. At some point, the Holy Spirit works in Bryan's heart, and he makes a decision to trust Christ.

5. *Integration into the church*: Tom is excited that Bryan has made a decision to become a Christian and he encourages Bryan to come to a program designed to deepen his new-found faith. This program, which we call Student Insight, meets on Sunday nights for the specific purpose of providing believers with opportunities to worship God, pray, learn from God's Word, and experience community with other Christians.

6. *Discipleship/small groups*: Bryan is invited to join a small group and experience further life change with five to eight of his peers in a small group setting. We call our small groups D-Teams ("D" stands for the Greek letter delta, a symbol for change). The purpose of D-Teams is to give students a chance to hold one another accountable in areas of life that need growth; to study God's Word on a deeper level; to pray for one another; and to develop a stronger sense of community.

7. *Ownership:* At this point, Bryan is ready and willing to give back to God by tithing and using his spiritual gift. At Student Impact, we encourage and challenge students to build the church by both giving of their resources and putting their spiritual gift into action. There are numerous serving opportunities in our ministry and our church, as well as mission trips to foreign countries and the inner-city. At this point, the process really does come full-cycle as Bryan starts to own the responsibility to repeat the cycle with one of his non-Christian friends.

If we're purposeful in our programming, we should be able to look at any program event and explain why we do it in light of our vision, mission, and strategy. Why do we have two programs a week, one on Tuesday and one on Sunday? Not because "we've always met on those nights," but because we have two distinct purposes to accomplish: reaching seekers and nurturing believers. (We'll talk more about this in chapter 4, on targets.) Why do we form small groups? Not because small groups are a growing trend these days, but because our purpose is to disciple students.

The bottom line is that everything in our ministries should be based on a God-given purpose. If we lose sight of our purpose, our ministries will stagnate and become program-driven rather than purpose-driven.

This is where the "rubber meets the road" in your planning. The reality of purpose is that you either have it or you don't. There is no middle ground. You and your team must take the time to answer that tough question, "Why?" about each program event. (In chapters 6 and 7 we'll talk about applying purposeful programming to the selection of the individual elements of each program event—for example, message topics, choice of music, and more.) Your efforts will be well repaid as you find yourselves making the most of every opportunity.

- Sit down with your calendar for the ministry season. For each scheduled program or event, answer the tough question, "Why?" See if each event fits with the vision and/or mission of your ministry.
- Categorize all your scheduled programs and events according to their purpose. A helpful way to do this is to break your vision statement into its component parts and use those as categories. For example, the vision statement for Student Impact is: "a unique community of students and leaders committed to letting God:

    change their lives;
    change their friends' lives;
    build the church; and
    impact the world."

    As I evaluate our programs, I can see how many have the purpose of reaching seekers whose lives need to be changed; how many have the purpose of equipping students to reach their friends; how many have the purpose of building the church; and how many have the purpose of helping students impact the world.

When you identify categories in this way, you might find that you have placed a high value in one area with a lot of programs planned for it but have neglected another area.

- When you're planning a program, you may come up with some great ideas but find they just don't fit that particular program's purpose. Everyone hates to "waste" a good idea, but resist the temptation to use it where it doesn't fit. Instead, make a file and save those ideas for possible use in future programs.
- Take a survey of your students and ask them what the purpose of a specific program is. You might be surprised!

more resources

Barna, George. *The Power of Vision*. Ventura, Calif.: Regal Books, 1992.

_____. *Turning Vision Into Action*. Ventura, Calif.: Regal Books, 1996.

Boshers, Bo. *Student Ministry for the 21st Century*. Grand Rapids: Zondervan, 1997.

Warren, Rick, *The Purpose Driven Church*. Grand Rapids: Zondervan, 1995.

# Warning!

The three steps you just read about—team, plan, and purpose—are the critical foundation upon which your programming ministry will be built. If you have not yet implemented these steps or taken action to do so, the rest of the material in this book will have nothing upon which to build. The first three steps really are a prerequisite before you can take your programs to the next level.

To determine if you should read on, answer the following questions:

- Do you have people organized into a team?
- Have you or will you in the near future do "big picture" planning well in advance of your actual programs?
- Can you identify the purpose of each particular scheduled program?

If you are ready, let's take a look at Phase Two: Target and Message.

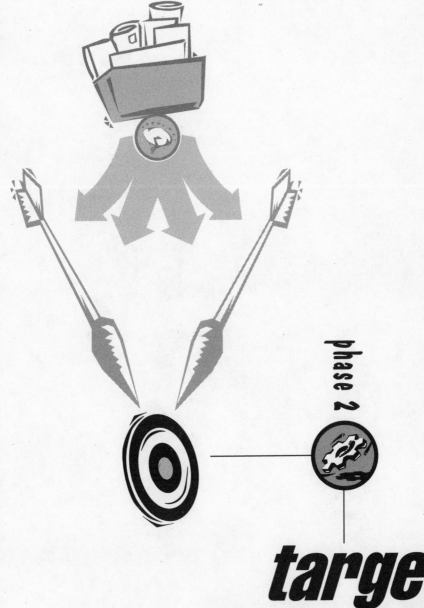

phase 2

target
message

# Step

# *target*

## If you aim at nothing, you will hit it every time

I served in the Marine Corps reserves for six years as an infantry soldier, otherwise known as a "grunt." Most people think I am crazy when I admit that I enjoyed my boot camp experience. It was a good time for me to get out on my own and learn a little about myself—and a lot more about discipline. Our platoon, like all of the others, spent twenty-four hours a day, seven days a week, for three months, practicing various drills, doing physical training, marching, and basically getting yelled at by three very angry drill instructors.

One of the drills that we spent hours practicing every day was disassembling, cleaning, and reassembling our M16-A1 rifles. We couldn't wait to have the chance to fire a real bullet through the chamber. At long last we were sent off the base to the firing range. We were pumped.

I vividly remember how we all expected to rush off of the bus onto the firing range, grab our buckets full of ammunition, and fire our rifles like soldiers in a typical Hollywood war movie. Instead, the drill instructors ordered us to sit down around a red steel barrel. They confidently explained that, before we could hit any targets on the range, we needed to become experts at what those targets looked like through the sights of our rifles.

On the barrel were painted several silhouettes of the target shapes in the sizes they would appear at different distances. For the next several hours, we aimed through the sights of our rifles at various targets without shooting, only looking and moving into the required firing positions. Our drill instructors taught us that you must be an expert at knowing the target in order to become an expert at hitting one. We had to do what I call the "barrel work" in order to know our target before attempting to hit it.

This discipline of knowing the target applies to programming as well. We need to remember that when we aim at nothing, we will probably hit just that. Many times, leaders will start "shooting at their audience" with a message or program without really knowing and understanding the target they are trying to hit. Shots fly out, but rarely do those shots hit the bull's-eye: reaching students for Jesus Christ.

As leaders in programming, we need to do our "barrel work" to understand the hearts and lives of those we seek to impact. The Marine Corps knew the stakes were too high for any recruit to be ignorant about what the target looked like. We, as soldiers of Christ, also need to know at what and at whom we are aiming—because the stakes for many are eternal.

## Who Are the Targets?

**tar•get** (tär′git) **n.** *One to be influenced* or *changed by an* **action** *or* **event**[1]

God knew when He wrote the Bible that it would need to reach all kinds of people. Every book of the Bible was originally written with a specific audience in mind. The apostle Paul was God's agent to write thirteen books in the New Testament, each targeted to a distinct group of people. The four gospels all share common stories about the life of Jesus Christ, but were written by four writers for various audiences with different needs: Matthew wrote to the Jews; Mark addressed the Christians in

Rome; Luke wrote to Theophilus and the Gentiles; and John targeted his book to new believers and searching nonbelievers.

Have you done your "barrel work" and taken the time to identify and get to know your target? If our desire is to paint an image of God for high school students, we must become a student of knowing our students' needs. Knowing these needs will impact what our programs look like. Let's take a brief look at each of five significant areas of adolescent development:

- physical
- intellectual
- emotional
- social
- spiritual

Obviously, adolescence is a time of tremendous physical growth and change as boys become young men and girls become young women. Hormones begin to run wild and physical and sexual changes, called puberty, cause tremendous growth spurts and the start of the sex drive. Effective programs must address the real cultural pressures students face from the media and advertisements, and students need to hear the issues of sexuality and boundaries addressed from a biblical viewpoint.

Intellectually, pre-adolescents are in what psychologist Jean Piaget termed the "concrete operational" stage: they are able to organize data but not conceptualize complex ideas. At about age twelve, students start moving into abstract thinking and formal reasoning. In this stage, students begin to understand more abstract concepts like "God is love." And by around age eighteen, students become idealistic thinkers and tend to look at issues as either black or white. Because of their different ways of looking at things, it is important to keep programs for junior high students different and apart from those for high school students. If you combine these two groups, your teaching will undoubtedly alienate some of your audience.

Emotions during adolescence can vary from hour to hour, minute to minute. Some of this emotional roller coaster is due to physical changes in students' bodies as well as social changes they are experiencing. Mood swings are to be expected during this time, but some adolescents suffer serious emotional problems, like suicidal thoughts, eating disorders, or depression. Learn the warning signs to look for. If you suspect one of your students has a serious problem, get help immediately.

But emotional development is not always traumatic. Students' hearts may be receptive to "moments" in your programs, like a heart-felt song or a real-life drama. While you shouldn't over-dramatize elements in your program just because you know your target may be more vulnerable, you can, through effective programming, move them toward God through their feelings and their hearts.

Social development is significant during adolescence as teens begin to develop their own identity apart from their parents and form bonds with their peers. Peer pressure really heats up as students are faced with different temptations and forced to make hard decisions. Many want so badly to fit in and be accepted that they may experiment with drugs, alcohol, or premarital sex. In planning programs, we need to address these issues that are stealing our students' lives.

At this stage of spiritual development, Christian students want their faith to be their own, not their parents' or grandparents' faith. They begin seeking and asking questions in order to inter-nalize and form their own beliefs. Non-Christian students, too, are seeking; they are looking for purpose and direction for their lives and wondering if God can provide them with that. Don't shrink back from teaching God's Word with boldness! Train your leader-ship to be prepared after programs to answer questions and provide spiritual direction for those who seek it.

Once we have an understanding of adolescent development, we can focus on specific targets. At Student Impact, we have three basic targets: those who desire to serve using the leadership gift God has given them (leaders); Christian students who are attempting to live as fully devoted followers (believers); and those students who don't know God but are searching (seekers). We are always working to know our targets better as we strive to develop programs that will meet each target's needs.

Leaders are looking for direction in three basic areas: infor-mation, care, and training. These three areas help them know what is expected of them and how they can serve most effectively. First, information is important so that they can better plan and stay on the same ministry page. No one likes being a part of something and not being informed. Second, it's also important for leaders to be cared for and to not feel used. Leaders must know that you are sincerely concerned for them and desire for them to win and grow in Christ. And finally, leaders need training so that their investment of time and energy can make a difference—no one wants to waste time being ineffective. Programs for leaders should include each of these areas so that they feel supported and encouraged to serve in your ministry.

Believers need to be taught from the Bible on a regular basis to grow them in the knowledge of God's Word and nurture their love for the church. They need to learn how to apply God's truth to their daily lives in order to grow in their faith. Believers also need a place where they can celebrate communion and worship God in community with other Christians. Because of these needs, programs for believers should include biblical teaching, worship, spiritual challenges, and communion.

Seekers are at a different place spiritually than believers, so we must think how to best minister to their situation. Seekers need to feel accepted and understood; they want someone to relate to their world. They want someone to respect the spiritual journey they are on and not pressure them to make any spiritual decisions until they are ready. They need to experience the power of the church. They may not realize it, but seekers long for purpose and meaning in their lives and wonder if God will fill the void in their souls. Seekers want a safe place to investigate God at their own pace. Programs for seekers should include spiritual challenges, elements that relate to their cultural world, and freedom to investigate Christianity without pressure.

We try to meet our targets' needs through different meetings and programs. For our leaders, we offer regular leadership meetings called 4uNet. And, as I mentioned in the last chapter, we offer two different programs, Student Impact (for seekers) and Student Insight (for believers). If we attempted to meet the needs of both targets within the same program events we would frustrate both believers and seekers, as well as ourselves.

As you think through and identify the specific targets and their different needs in your ministry, remember to take another look at your ministry's purpose. What have you decided your ministry will be about and how does that affect whom you will target? Effective ministry can happen for all of us if we take the time to do our barrel work and know who we are trying to reach with a particular program.

## Why Target?

*"When the archer misses the mark, he turns and looks for the fault within himself. Failure to hit the bull's-eye is never the fault of the target."*

GILBERT ARLAND[2]

Every fall, I look forward to purchasing my bow-hunter's license. My father-in law, John, and his buddy John L., were responsible for teaching me how to hunt deer. Basically, they handed me a bow and some arrows and figured I'd learn the rest along the way. They did give me one golden rule that, if I stuck to it, would greatly increase my chances of actually hitting my target. The rule was to "pick a spot." No matter what you do, they advised, make sure you pick out the exact spot you are attempting to hit. At the time, it seemed so obvious that I really didn't pay much attention—until I saw my first deer from the tree stand.

As the deer came into range, my heart was pumping so hard I nearly fell out of the tree. I pulled back the arrow on my bow with great quickness, forgetting to follow the "golden rule," and in a rush of adrenaline, I let it fly. I would have missed an elephant if it had been ten feet in front of me! Once again I was reminded of the saying, "If you aim at nothing, you will hit it every time."

One of the most common programming pitfalls I see in student ministry is stuffing anybody and everybody into the same room, tossing around some "half-baked" program elements with no real order, and hoping to meet the needs of all those attending. It's a shock that students ever come back to experiences like that!

In a bad program with several targets, we may hit some people, but we will probably do more damage than good. Leaders', believers', and seekers' needs are not best met using the shotgun method because each group's needs are very different.

Another danger we face when we don't consciously "pick a spot" is overlooking the seeker target. Unless we consciously target certain programs specifically to seekers, we can easily spend most of our time and effort ministering to the already convinced. We need to spend time growing our leaders and believers, but we must put an equal amount of energy into planning programs for seekers. We must never forget that our churches or ministries are not to be museums for saints, but hospitals for sinners.

## How Do You Target?

"Man is always inclined to be intolerant toward the thing, or person, he hasn't taken time to understand."

Robert R. Brown[3]

My Marine Corps platoon did barrel work for several days. In fact, we only fired our weapons for two days out of the two weeks we were at the firing range. We were sore and tired from lying down and sitting in various positions, but it all proved worthwhile: our seventy-man platoon had an almost one hundred percent qualifying rate for badges. Little did we realize that it wasn't purely a result of gifted riflemen, but mostly of the discipline of understanding our targets.

We student ministers need to discipline ourselves to do our own kind of barrel work. It is not always fun and it can be hard work. But it, too, will prove worth the effort when our programs hit the mark and reach our targets. Two disciplines I have found useful in helping learn more about targets are interviewing and research.

One way to understand your targets is to interview them. Go to the source. Set up a meeting with a few believers from your ministry and a different meeting with several seekers, either from your ministry or from a local high school. With each group, ask as much as you can about who they are, what they like and don't like, their family and church backgrounds, their interests, and what's current in their world. Find out what life is like for high school students of today's generation. Focus on the struggles and victories they currently face in their lives, because that is where the door to their hearts will most likely be.

Ask the seekers if they go to church regularly. If not, why? What turns them off about Christianity? What would motivate them to go to a church? Try to discover what needs they have and if your current programs are meeting them. Ask the believers what they need in order to grow in their walk with Christ. What challenges and peer pressure do they face taking a stand for Christ on their campus? How can your ministry best encourage and support them?

It might be a good idea to organize these meetings throughout the ministry year with different students to keep learning more about your targets. You and your programming team will benefit as you become students of your students.

As for researching your targets, you'll find many books about adolescent development in the local library and bookstores. (I've listed some helpful books in the resource section at the end of this chapter.) Our team is always reading or researching what the issues are for students today so that we never get "stuck" in our ministry. Even though this will cost your team a fair amount of time, it is a great discipline to encourage them to do on a regular basis.

Secular magazine racks can also provide current information on cultural issues. Magazines are useful because they may provide topic ideas for programs relevant to issues in the student culture. However, some of the magazines out there will be more hurtful to you than helpful, so be careful.

You can also research your targets by going where they go. Remember how much time you spent "hanging out"? The places may have changed, but the habit is the same: students go where students are. One place that is popular with our students is the mall. Credit cards have given today's students more financial privileges and encouraged them to do whatever is necessary to look and dress "right." It is interesting to observe what students are wearing, the latest hairstyles, and what kinds jewelry they are buying. Many stores in the mall market to high school students, so look closely at store windows to discover what appeals to students today.

Once you interview and research your targets, you'll have lots of information to help you effectively minister to the students in your area. From there, you and your team need to determine how to best use the information you have gathered and incorporate it into your programs. For example, what music do your targets listen to? Imagine if a seeker walked into a program and heard a song that he or she knew! Instead of thinking, *These people are weird,* the student will think, *These people understand me and know what I like!* This makes them more tuned into the message and receptive to hearing about Christ.

God does the work, but we as His agents may only have one opportunity, one shot, to reach a soul. Unless we are focused and know who our students are, where they come from, or what they are about, we may miss. Like Paul in the New Testament, who worked hard to know where people were at in order to deliver the truth of Jesus Christ, we are responsible to give our best effort to know our target audience. If you understand whom a program is for, you can more effectively design the program so that meaningful ministry can take place. You have "picked your spot" and, with God's help, can hit the target!

*try this . . .*

- Here are some questions about targets to think through:

    Who on your team is researching students? Who is interviewing? How often is research and interviewing happening?

    How broad is the age group you are trying to reach? Do you offer a separate program for junior high students? If not, why not?

    What music do your targets listen to? What TV shows do they watch?

    Where are the local hangouts in your area?

What demographics—race, socio-economic status, geographic location—may influence your programming?

- Talk with other student ministers in your area. What works in their ministries? What kinds of programs do they offer?
- Subscribe to a few youth magazines popular with your target so that you know what is current in their world. A few student favorites: *Rolling Stone, Sports Illustrated, Glamour, Cosmopolitan, Details,* and *Wired.*
- Check if your local police department, hospital, high school, or community center offers any seminars on working with adolescents. The information offered might be helpful, and you may make some key contacts with other youth workers.
- Sit down and get feedback and stories from an adolescent counselor in your area.
- If you haven't already done so, divide junior high students from high school students and offer separate programs for each group.
- Work with students' emotional development by providing opportunities after programs for students to talk with other students and share their feelings. This can most effectively be done through a ministry of small groups. You can also encourage students to open up with one another through interactive teaching. Have students sit around tables and, at different points during the message, stop and give students a few questions to discuss.
- Capitalize on the importance of peers by letting students teach students. Use student testimonies or stories to support the truth conveyed in a program. Stories from peers can often be the most effective element in a program.

*more resources*

Barna, George. *Generation Next.* Ventura, Calif.: Regal Books, 1995.
Celek, Tim, and Dieter Zander. *Inside the Soul of a New Generation.* Grand Rapids: Zondervan, 1996.
Coupland, Douglas. *Life After God.* New York: Pocket Books, 1994.

Grossberg, Lawrence, ed. *Cultural Studies.* New York: Routledge, 1991.

McDowell, Josh and Bob Hostetler. *Right From Wrong.* Dallas: Word, 1994.

_____. *Josh McDowell's Handbook on Counseling Youth.* Dallas: Word, 1996.

Mueller, Walt. *Understanding Today's Youth Culture.* Wheaton, Ill.: Tyndale, 1994.

Olson, Dr. G. Keith. *Counseling Teenagers.* Loveland, Colo.: Group Books, 1984.

Popcorn, Faith. *The Popcorn Report.* New York: Doubleday, 1991.

Rowley, William. *Equipped to Care.* Wheaton, Ill.: Victor Books, 1990.

Strobel, Lee. *Inside the Mind of Unchurched Harry and Mary.* Grand Rapids: Zondervan, 1993.

Student Impact Leadership Conference tape on adolescent development, available through the Willow Creek Association (847) 765-0070.

# Step 5

# message

## Don't make your message mean something; teach something meaningful

The Thursday-night prime-time television series lineup of *Friends, The Single Guy, The Naked Truth, Seinfeld,* and *E.R.* has been dubbed "Must See TV" that hundreds of thousands of people change their schedules to watch. What exactly is it that we "must see?" One episode on *Friends* shows Ross trying to figure out how to parent his young son, who at the moment is being raised by his lesbian mother who is "married" to her lesbian girlfriend. In another episode, we heard of Chandler's sexual escapades with his girlfriend of the month. As if that weren't enough, Monica and Rachel then fight over who gets the last condom in their medicine cabinet while their boyfriends wait naked in bed for them.

*Seinfeld*'s cast of characters are another interesting bunch. George is shown almost every week interacting with his dysfunctional parents and is always trying to figure out how to have a sexual relationship without a commitment. In a recent episode, Elaine asks for sexual advice from Jerry because she is having trouble with her current boyfriend's sexual performance. And Kramer, Jerry's crazy neighbor, is hardly a role model of a well-adjusted, responsible adult!

Obviously, Hollywood sends out a worldly, hedonistic message along with an egocentric set of morals and beliefs. Many of the people who create these "must see" shows do not know the Source of truth, life, grace, and love. They do not have the message we are so privileged to share! The truly sad part of this reality is that our young people today watch more television than ever. What message are they hearing and watching? What must they see?

I hope you and your team realize that you have been entrusted to deliver the most powerful message known to humankind: the transforming love of Jesus Christ. When you have planned your programs, determined their purpose, and learned about the needs of your target, you are ready to decide what message to teach and how to prepare that message.

## What Is a Message?

 **mes•sage** (mes'ij) n. A communication divinely inspired or embodying important principles or counsel[1]

Being a native southern Californian, I've experienced a number of earthquakes. Some of them have been small and weak, shaking only the pictures on our walls, while a few earthquakes caused major damage. It was always amazing to drive around the neighborhood after a big earthquake. Often, the old homes and buildings, which seemed so weak, were still standing, while the new homes and buildings were leveled by the force of the quake. Underneath all of the weather-beaten exteriors lay the reason a home stood or fell: the foundation. The homes still standing had foundations that were built strong and designed to resist such power. But the homes built carelessly or with flaws had foundations that could not withstand a major quake. Obviously, structures without solid foundations will not last.

If an earthquake rocked one of your programs, what would be left standing? Upon what have you built your programs? How strong is the foundation of each of your programs? The message is the foundation on which the entire program is built. Without a good message, programs will be weak and susceptible to becoming just entertainment.

Programs should be designed to support the message by setting the speaker up to communicate God's truth. A foundational message from the word of God will give strength to the whole program. The life-changing message of Jesus Christ will always stand!

What exactly should a message look like? It may be helpful to start off describing what a message is *not*.

First, a message is not a stand-up comedy routine. Too often, I have observed speakers trying so hard to be liked by their audience that they become entertainers. Instead of teaching about Christ, they tell funny stories to make their audience laugh and never really get to the gospel message. In many cases, this type of communication comes from a person who has a deep need for acceptance rather than a desire to speak truth. There is a place for the use of humor in teaching, but it must never overshadow what God has called us to proclaim, His message with boldness and without apology. In his book *The Power of Story*, evangelist Leighton Ford warns, "Jesus did not intend His church merely to provide bigger and better amusement for bigger and more upscale audiences. His Vision was of a church that would inject His light and life into a dark and dying world. So we had better take the Vision of Jesus seriously, or we won't just be amusing ourselves to death. We'll be amusing people to hell."[2]

Second, a message is not based on our ideas or opinions, but on God's Word. Sometimes it's tempting to spiritualize our ideas by saying, "Here's a cool idea that students will like. Now let's just find the right verses." Rather, our teaching should originate from God's Word and what the Holy Spirit is telling us. After that, we can brainstorm creative ideas to add life to our presentation. An unknown author said, "The one who uses the Bible as a guide will never lose his sense of direction."

And finally, a message is not a lecture. Have you ever listened to a message-giver who sounded more like a prison warden? God never intended for His Truth to sound or to feel like punishment. Or have you heard a message-giver who sounded more like a "know-it-all" professor who belonged in a university setting? God wants His Truth to be understood and communicated no matter what the audience's education level. Remember the last time you witnessed an audience fall asleep, one by one, as the message-giver droned on and on? That should never happen during a message. God's Truth is exciting and full of life!

God has chosen those of us who teach to be the voice box for His message. It's not our message; we are simply His messengers.

We have an opportunity to paint an image of God by sharing how He has or is working in a particular area of our lives, things He has taught us, passions He has given us, and what He has revealed to us.

God uses His Holy Spirit to change and mold our hearts and minds in order to reveal a "real-life" message to our audience. You can see why it is so important ,when we are given the responsibility to preach the Word, that we also be in the Word. Theologian John Stott states, "The Scripture comes alive to the congregation [in our case, student ministry] only if it has come alive to the preacher first."[3] We must not only be authentic communicators, but also be willing to receive the message ourselves.

Not only is message-giving about sharing our hearts and what God is revealing to us, it also involves discerning the real and felt needs of our audience. What is happening in the world and in students' schools and communities? What issues must we address? It's a challenge to keep up on the ever-changing student culture and world. How can we best teach about current events in a relevant, biblical way? Leighton Ford states, "Jesus didn't just focus on His message, on making His point. He focused on people, on their feelings, on their needs, on their issues, on their healing. He made people feel valued and loved. And so should we."[4] Meeting our audience's needs is a continual challenge as we teach them truth that can change their eternity!

Students want and need to hear the truth. They face numerous struggles, and many of them wrestle with tough questions. Those questions will never get answered without God's message. We can help our students by teaching them about Jesus Christ, who is the answer for which many of them are searching.

## Why Is the Message So Important?

> "A CREDIBLE MESSAGE NEEDS A CREDIBLE MESSENGER BECAUSE CHARISMA WITHOUT CHARACTER IS CATASTROPHIC."

PETER KUZMIC[5]

What kind of messages are getting through to high school students today? In the beginning of this chapter, I mentioned a few messages being communicated through television. Students watch an average of twenty-two hours of télévision a week. By the time a child graduates from high school, he or she will have watched about twenty-three thousand hours of television as compared with the eleven thousand hours spent in the school classroom.[6] This equals over two and a half years of nonstop television messages our students are receiving!

MTV has become a cultural phenomenon. Studies indicate that the average teen watches somewhere between thirty minutes and two hours of music videos a day.[7] In other words, while in high school, students will watch an average of fifty-six twenty-four hours days of MTV. A 1992 study reported that an average of 12.5 violent scenes per hour are shown on MTV alone.[8] Using the average of viewing MTV one hour a day, students will watch 16,800 violent acts by the time they graduate—and this is on just one cable station!

In addition, most teenagers listen to four to six hours of music daily. The reality is that students will listen to 1,680 hours of music, which equals seventy days, in one year. In *Understanding Today's Youth Culture*, Walt Mueller writes, "Music has become one of the most effective teachers, preachers, and evangelists of our time. Its power lies in its ability to define reality and shape world and life views. And its messages are providing a sound track for a generation that is being molded in the image of music itself."[9] That's a frightening statement, because much of the music molding students today carries far from a saving message. Observers of the pop music scene contend, "If you tune in to one of those [radio] stations, you'll hear about everything from numbness and alienation, sour relationships, cynicism and pain."[10]

But we don't have to surrender to the influence of popular music, music videos, and television programs. There is power in the spoken word. Who could forget Martin Luther King's famous "I Have a Dream" speech, spoken with such conviction and passion? Or the power of Billy Graham's gospel messages to move millions around the world?

These well-known communicators made sure their messages were heard because they believed strongly in their cause. They were convinced that what they had to say was urgent and timely. As leaders in student ministry, we too have good news to share. The verbal proclamation of the Truth of Christ is a message that is timeless and can benefit every person on the planet.

God knew that verbal communication would impact people's souls. Look at a few verses from the Bible that use "hearing" as the key word:

> Therefore everyone who hears these words of mine and puts them into practice is like a wise man who built his house on the rock (Matt. 7:24).
> He who has ears, let him hear (Matt. 11:15).
> My sheep listen to my voice; I know them, and they follow me (John 10:27).
> How, then, can they call on the one they have not believed in? And how can they believe in the one of whom they have not heard? And how can they hear without someone preaching to them? (Rom. 10:14)

Even though we live in a society that is saturated with sin and mixed messages, there is still an audience receptive to listening to the message we have been called to communicate. Let's communicate it often, clearly, and with boldness!

## How Do You Prepare a Message?

> ❝Your ability to practice what you preach brings power to what you preach. Pastors, youth workers, and Sunday School teachers are providing a constant message with their lives. If that message is inconsistent with the message that they preach, then the power of their communication is greatly diminished.❞ **ken davis** [11]

I cannot give you a quick and easy set of steps to prepare messages. That's God's work in and through you. He speaks to each of us in different ways and leads us to communicate His Word in various styles. Many people have suggestions on how to prepare messages; I encourage you to read any of the additional resources listed at the end of this chapter. Ken Davis, for example, in his book *How to Speak to Youth*, teaches that you must include personal preparation, objective preparation, and physical preparation. Personally, I have found it helpful to focus on four areas: (1) retreat; (2) research; (3) rewrite; and (4) rehearse.

First, I believe it is important to *retreat* and find time to be alone with God. Effective ministry begins with quietness. It is in those quiet moments with the Lord that we will be able to listen to His voice and hear what He is saying to us. By slowing down the pace of our lives and blocking out any interruptions, we can begin to be still and know that He is God (Ps. 46:10). God knows what our students need to hear, and will reveal that to us when we quiet ourselves before Him. What we teach our students can then flow out of what God is teaching us.

Sometimes it is easy to get so busy "doing" the work of God that the work of God is hardly present in our daily lives. Our role in student ministry should never negate God's work in us. I usually try to get away from the pace of life, my work schedule, my "to do" lists, and other people, for a two- to five-hour block of time once a week. I do this for the purpose of getting quiet, reading, praying, and trying to identify the message God has used in my life and wants me to share.

The second step in preparing a message is to *research*. The first place to study is God's Word. It is the one true source from which our messages should evolve. Additional resources and personal experience will add life to the way we present the biblical truth. Possible illustration resources include books, magazines, newspapers, the Internet, and other people. Leighton Ford counsels, "Instead of telling the gospel Story by expounding and exegeting the biblical texts in a sentence-by-sentence fashion, we must bring the truth of God alive just as Jesus did, with stories, parables, word pictures, and vivid metaphors."[12] Often, our own personal anecdotes can be the most effective illustrations.

Take time to read the biblical passage on which you are teaching. Write down any possible study areas that may help you better understand the passage. Then go to places with multiple study resources available, like a library or bookstore, to research your topic. Try to research as much as you can so you feel knowledgeable and have plenty of material. The rule of thumb I like to follow is to research enough so that I have a larger understanding than what I will need to teach. I want to understand what I am teaching so well that I could give the message without my notes.

Third, it is important to write and *rewrite* your message. Remember that old classroom punishment of rewriting "I will not _____" on the blackboard? That disciplinary action really works! The more a message is rewritten, the better it will become. Write out your message word-for-word, especially if you're fairly new at this. If you really feel that writing out the message doesn't fit your personal style, then at least write a detailed speaking outline that will chart a course for your message. As you go through this process, you will be able to refine your thoughts and communicate a clearer message.

Lastly, *rehearse, rehearse, rehearse.* Practice your message in the mirror; record it on tape, shoot it on video—anything that will give you an opportunity to hear what you are going to say and make needed adjustments. Rehearse as many times as it takes in order to know your material well enough so you don't experience "note bondage." You want everyone who listens to your message to hear your heart, not just a bunch of written notes.

Leighton Ford summed up the task set before all message-givers: "That is the challenge before you and me as storytellers of God's grace: As we tell and live out His Story in our daily lives, we must make the grace and truth of Jesus Christ so vivid that it can be seen and touched by the minds and imaginations of the people around us."[13]

*try this . . .*

- Schedule one day a week to retreat, research, rewrite, and rehearse. Don't start working on a message the night before you are to give it. If possible, work at least four to six weeks in advance.

- Build a file of message thoughts or teachable moments that you encounter through life experiences so you have a library of illustrations from which to draw.
- Journal your thoughts and prayers on a daily or weekly basis.
- Attend a message preparation seminar or class. I recommend the Dynamic Communicators Workshop by Ken Davis. For further information, write Dynamic Communications International, P.O. Box 745940, Arvada, CO 80006, or call 303–425–1319.
- Find a teacher or pastor you respect to meet with you on a regular basis for coaching on communication skills.

**more resources**

Davis, Ken. *How to Speak to Youth*. Loveland, Colo.: Group Publishing, 1986.

_____. *Secrets of Dynamic Communication*. Grand Rapids: Zondervan, 1991.

Ford, Leighton. *The Power of Story*. Colorado Springs: NavPress, 1994.

Hybels, Bill, Haddon Robinson, and Stuart Briscoe. *Mastering Contemporary Preaching*. Portland, Ore.: Multnomah, 1989.

Levine, Mark L., and Eugene Rachlis. *The Complete Book of Bible Quotations*. New York: Pocket Books, 1986.

Pitt-Watson, Ian. *A Primer for Preachers*. Grand Rapids: Baker Book House, 1986.

Robinson, Haddon W. *Biblical Preaching*. Grand Rapids: Baker Book House, 1980.

Sproul, R. C. *Knowing Scripture*. Downers Grove, Ill.: InterVarsity Press, 1977.

Stott, John. *The Preacher's Portrait*. Grand Rapids: Eerdmans, 1961.

_____. *Between Two Worlds: The Art of Preaching in the 20th Century*. Grand Rapids: Eerdmans, 1982.

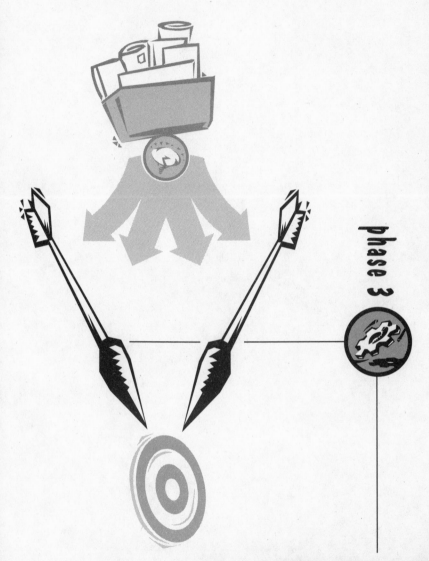

phase 3

**rationale
direction**

# Step 6 rationale

## What are you trying to say?

I will never forget my first sailing experience. I was invited to a week-long sailing trip in the British Virgin Islands with four friends from the church staff. We arrived on the island of Tortola to board the boat and meet Tom, our captain for the week. He gave us a quick lesson on sailing and each of us received an assignment.

As we started to sail, I asked Tom, "Where are we going?" He pointed out to a very small spot on the horizon that he assured me was an island. He told me how we were going to get there and how long it was going to take. Although I didn't realize it at the time, Tom had charted our course for the week, island to island, with a compass and a map. He knew exactly where he wanted to take us and had made up his mind on how we were going to get there.

When we look at our programs, we need to ask: "Where is this program going? What is its end destination?" Stephen Covey, in his book *The 7 Habits of Highly Effective People*, states, "To begin with the end in mind means to start with a clear understanding of your destination. It means to know where you're going so that you better understand where you are now and so that the steps you take are always in the right direction."[1]

How many message-givers have found themselves lost and unsure of where they were going while giving a message? How many program directors have felt that their creative program isn't taking the audience where it was originally planned to go? It doesn't take long to find out what I mean. Just ask a few of your listeners what they heard and then observe how close it is to what you intended them to hear. Where did they end up? Message-giving and programs need to have a clear, carefully chosen route and an end destination in mind in order to communicate God's truth effectively. Before starting the message and program development process, the message-giver and program director need to use a "map" to organize a clear presentation of God's Word. This map is called a rationale statement.

## What Is a Rationale Statement?

 ra•tion•ale **(rash'en-al') n.**
The *rational* or **logical** basis of **something**[2]

Speaker Ken Davis defines rationale as "the points of logic that will lead to the objective.... The rationale establishes a logical foundation upon which the credibility of your speech will rest."[3] A rationale statement provides purpose and focus and keeps the speaker from getting lost during preparation and delivery of the message. It points the message in the right direction and keeps it on course.

At Student Impact, our rationale statements include the big picture (a brief summary of the message); a propositional state- ment (the message thesis and the main points of the message); the Scripture text; and any ideas that could assist the message- giver. Every series has an overall rationale statement of what we want students to learn or understand. Within the series, each week has its own specific rationale. We require a message-giver to turn in a rationale statement for each message approximately four to six weeks before the program. If the speaker is doing a series over a few weeks, then he or she turns in rationale statements for the entire series.

Here's an example of the rationale we used for a recent series on friendship called "Real Friends":

# October 29: "What Are Real Friends?"

**Big Picture:** We would all probably say that we have friendships, but many of us could probably not answer where those friendships stand. Will your friendships stand the test of time and adversity, or are they surface friendships that won't last beyond this month? In this session, we will look at a friendship gauge that, if read properly, will help us know where our friendships stand.

**Propositional Statement:** Every one of us can know where our friendships are at by looking at three levels on the gauge of friendships.

#1: Cold
#2: Lukewarm
#3: Hot or "redline"

**Scripture:** Proverbs 18:24, 17:17; Ecclesiastes 4:9–12
**Ideas:** It would be great to have on stage as a prop a big gauge that could move from cold to hot.

# November 5: "Real Friends Build"

**Big Picture:** Anything of great value in life usually costs much time and effort. Friendships are valuable and require time and effort to build. One key building block in strengthening our friendships is encouragement. This evening will cover two ways someone could encourage a friend.

**Propositional Statement:** Every one of us can build our friendships by looking at two basic areas of encouragement:

Area #1: Who our friends are (Encouraging the inside character of someone)
Area #2: Where they are going (Encouraging where they are going and what they are doing)

**Scripture:** Hebrews 3:13
**Ideas:** Use a stage prop such as a large jar full of miscellaneous items in it like cards, rocks, marbles, action figures, music CD, toothbrush, etc. This prop could be used as an illustration of how

someone might begin to look for what is inside a person rather than what is on the outside.

## November 12: "Real Friends Sharpen"

**Big Picture:** Relationships are not always easy. In fact, they can be rough and take a whole lot of work. We will look at what God has to say about real friends: "As iron sharpens iron, so one man sharpens another" (Prov. 27:17).

**Propositional Statement:** Real friends can sharpen each other by committing to two important values:

Value #1: Tell the truth—the lost art of honesty.
Value #2: Take the high road—How much does your friendship matter? Choosing to work through the conflict and not taking the easy way out.

**Scripture:** Proverbs 24:26; Matthew 18:15; Proverbs 27:17
**Ideas:** It would be great to have a drama or a movie clip of someone telling the truth to a good friend.

## November 19: "Real Friends Stay"

**Big Picture:** Every one of us is disappointed by friends. We sometimes wonder if there are really any "real friends" anywhere. In our final week of the series, we will see how God wants to, and can be, the ultimate Friend we are all looking for.

**Propositional Statement:** Every one of us tonight can have God as our real friend by making two simple decisions:

Decision #1: To accept His friendship and His offer of love and salvation
Decision #2: To trust in His council and give Him every part of our life

**Scripture:** John 3:16; Proverbs 3:5–6
**Ideas:** This evening will be a decision night, so anything with the arts that will paint a picture of what it would be like to live life without God as a real friend. Communicate the emotion of loneliness.

# Why Have a Rationale Statement?

 "No horse gets anywhere until he is harnessed. No steam or gas ever drives anything until it is confined. No Niagara is ever turned into light and power until it is tunneled. No life ever grows great until it is focused, dedicated, disciplined."

**HARRY EMERSON FOSDICK**[4]

I spent the early years of my life around horses. My responsibilities were to feed and give them water daily. After some time, my father felt I was ready to have a horse of my own. I'll never forget that day he called me to the corral. I ran outside and saw my father standing at the fence pointing to a new young pony. He said, "It's yours."

My dad suggested I try him out, so I climbed on—only to find out that the pony hadn't been broken in. After picking myself up off of the ground, I learned that the pony needed a bridle to harness its young energy.

Message-givers and programs can be just like a wild horse, powerful and dangerous. Both need a "bridle" to harness and focus their energy toward one specific purpose. Incorporating a rationale statement in your programming development process can be the bridle that will give your message-givers and programs a focused energy that can make a greater impact.

A well-thought-out rationale statement will provide focus in a number of ways. First, a clearly-stated rationale statement for a message can become a great source of accountability as you develop your overall program package. You will no longer have those "cross your fingers, close your eyes, and hope that the program and the message-giver say something meaningful" kinds of experiences. A good rationale statement prevents a message-giver from "winging it" and the program from becoming a disconnected thought.

Speaker Ken Davis states:

> If you have no focused objective for your talk, how can you expect the audience to know what you are talking about? In the first few moments of your speech the audience is deciding

whether you have anything important to say. If they discern that there is no direction or focus to your talk, you might as well pack your bags and go home because that's what their minds will do.[5]

Second, having a clear rationale helps message-givers guard against the "too much material, not enough time" syndrome. Sometimes even the best speakers are tempted to share all their life lessons and knowledge—in one thirty-minute message! It is far better to give listeners just enough so that they are able to comprehend what is being communicated. Dr. Bruce H. Wilkinson, in his workshop "Seven Laws of the Learner," uses this statement as a pledge: "I commit to cause my students to master the minimum." Articulating the message rationale keeps the speaker focused on the essentials so that the audience can understand what is being communicated.

Third, spelling out the rationale of a message provides just enough information to help focus the creative ideas in a program and to minimize wasted efforts. Creative thinkers need boundaries to keep their artistic passions focused. It is unrealistic in most cases for the message-giver to hand over his or her entire message, word for word, to the programming team on a regular basis weeks before they give it, but a simple outline of the message will provide the necessary boundaries to determine what and where program elements like music, video, testimony, or drama should be used in order to support the message.

Using a rationale statement to plan programs helps the message-giver and your programming team work more efficiently and effectively. If you are familiar with any team-building experience, you know that team members need to understand why they are doing what they are doing. And if you have worked with creative people, you realize that they have high levels of energy when it comes to producing an exciting idea and need a set of boundaries for their time and energy. Our Student Impact programming team regularly has to draw these boundaries. We have been blessed with many gifted people and incredible resources. Occasionally, we have caught ourselves in a planning meeting, building and developing an idea, only to end up going back to the program's rationale statement to see if the idea fits. We often end up admitting to each other,

"This idea will not take the program where we want it to go," "It doesn't fit," or "It's not worth the time and energy."

## How Do You Create a Rationale Statement?

**"WE NEED TO PREPARE SIMPLE POINTS OF LOGIC THAT WILL LEAD US IN THE RIGHT DIRECTION."**

*Ken Davis*[6]

As I mentioned in the last chapter, the message preparation process begins with retreating and being quiet before the Lord. During this time, He will begin to reveal to you what your target needs to hear. Once a message-giver has been given the message it will not be very difficult to write out a simple statement of purpose. Remember: The message-giver should try to create the rationale statement by writing a thesis sentence to show direction (where will the message go?) and also the main points to communicate (what will the target learn?). Here are a few things to remember in creating a rationale statement.

First, the rationale statement should be brief and concise. One phrase I picked up while coaching high school football teams was, "Keep It Simple, Stupid." That phrase became a reminder to us as coaches to remember that it is better to master a few of the basics than to be average in all of them. Rationale statements should communicate a simple truth.

Second, once the message-giver has a first draft of the rationale, he or she may find it beneficial to ask a couple of people to assist in fine-tuning the statement. These people can affirm what has been developed thus far or offer suggestions and ideas of other possible angles to take. Let me warn you: this is not easy to do or be a part of, although it is a process that will help a message-giver let go of some pride and become more coachable, and will create an environment where everyone in the room can let go of his or her agenda and allow the Holy Spirit to work with them, together.

Third, agree on what the rationale statement will look like. Determine what is effective for you and your team. One approach we have used is one our senior pastor, Bill Hybels, has recommended. He asks two basic questions: "What do I want the audience to *know*?" and "What do I want the audience to *do*?" Answering these two questions on paper is one way to create an effective rationale statement for a message.

Another popular approach to rationale and message preparation is Ken Davis' SCORRE method. SCORRE stands for: Subject; Central theme; Objective; Rationale; Resources; and Evaluation. Using this outline gives sharp focus to what is being communicated and may assist you and your team in developing purposeful programs. This method is explained in his two books listed in the resources section at the end of this chapter. At Student Impact, our rationale statements incorporate the "O" (the propositional statement) and the "R" (the main points of the message).

The method you use to develop rationale statements is up to you and your team. What is important is to recognize the value of incorporating this step into message and program preparation. If you ask for God's intervention and direction, He will surely provide it, and articulating the rationale statement will become a fruitful part of your programming process. Leave it out and you will find yourself in meetings and programs that lack the focus and effectiveness to affect someone's eternity.

*try this . . .*

- Schedule a rationale development meeting each week and invite those people whom you feel will contribute suggestions and ideas. Try to finalize the rationale statement for a message at least two or three weeks in advance.
- When our team gets stuck developing a rationale statement, we write out what we have so far on a flip chart or dry-erase board. Seeing ideas visually as you brainstorm will assist your team in making the rationale statements clear and simple.
- After a program, ask some of your regular and new listeners what they heard from the message and also what they learned from the program as a whole.

- Practice writing rationale statements for every meeting, message, or presentation. They will help you pinpoint the purpose for your message or the reason for the meeting. (You may even eliminate some meetings!)

more resources

Buechner, Frederick. *Telling the Truth: The Gospel as Tragedy, Comedy, and Fairy Tale*. San Francisco: Harper & Row, 1977.
Davis, Ken. *How to Speak to Youth*. Loveland, Colo.: Group Books, 1986.
_____. *Secrets of Dynamic Communication*. Grand Rapids: Zondervan, 1991.
Nash, Ronald H. *The Word of God and the Mind of Man*. Grand Rapids: Zondervan, 1982.
*Story Telling Magazine*, National Story Telling Association, P.O. Box 309, Jonesbourgh, Tennessee 37659.

# Step 7

# *direction*

## Choose the route

One of my favorite memories from when I was a kid is of taking road trips. I can still remember the early-morning departures and late-evening arrivals. Even today, I still enjoy road trips. Our family takes several trips a year to my in-laws' home in Wisconsin. One of the decisions Tricia and I have to make before we leave is which route to take. From our home, there are several ways to make the trip, but we have worked our list down to two basic routes we use most often. On one of the routes, we drive through several towns and make numerous fast-food stops, which makes the trip feel shorter. This route seems easier and quicker, but actually it takes longer.

On the other route, we travel sixty-five miles per hour the entire way. There are only a few stops and even fewer towns, but lots of barns and beautiful countryside. This trip feels longer and can be harder with the kids, but in the end it is a much quicker route. Two different routes. Two different experiences. The same destination.

Let me illustrate this in another way. Imagine that you have been promoted to the position of marketing director for a brand-new clothing line targeted at students ages fifteen to nineteen. Your first responsibility is to create and direct a sixty-second television commercial. The president doesn't care how you market the product, only that students buy it. You begin to brainstorm dozens of different ways you could make students feel excited about your product. You might play into the feeling that they must have your product to be "in" with their friends, or you might try the angle that a better product does not exist. There are many possibilities, many different angles. The same objective.

In programming, we can take many different directions in addressing a particular topic. Psychologists have discovered that humans are capable of four basic emotions; we either feel glad, mad, sad, or scared. All other emotions stem from these four emotions. The route of emotion we take will change the complexion and tone of the program, but every route should end up at the same destination.

## What Is Direction?

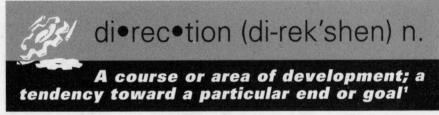

di•rec•tion (di-rek'shen) n.

*A course or area of development; a tendency toward a particular end or goal*[1]

When we talk about "direction" at Student Impact, we mean the emotional road the program takes. For example, let's refer back to our sample rationale statement for week four of the "Real Friends" series:

### November 19: "Real Friends Stay"

**Big Picture:** Every one of us is disappointed by friends. We sometimes wonder if there are any "real friends" anywhere. In our final week of the series, we will see how God wants to, and can be, the ultimate Friend we are all looking for.

**Propositional Statement:** Every one of us tonight can have God as our real friend by making two simple decisions:

Decision #1: To accept His friendship and His offer of love and salvation

Decision #2: To trust in His council and give Him every part of our life

**Scripture:** John 3:16; Proverbs 3:5–6

What road would you choose to take in planning this program? A possible direction might be to convey the feelings students have when they lack authentic friendships and feel abandoned. This direction may evoke feelings of sadness, hurt, betrayal, or loneliness. Another possible direction would be to focus on friendships that stay with you for life, especially a friendship with God. The emotions in this program could include happiness, acceptance, and security. In setting the direction for this program, we chose to go with the second, more positive route.

The emotional tone you decide to set will affect the kinds of programming elements you choose to use. For every program you plan, you need to determine the emotional direction it will take and the appropriate programming elements to use to achieve the desired goal. For example, in the first scenario, you most likely would not want to use a funny, encouraging kind of drama or an upbeat song. This is what Willow Creek Programming Director Nancy Beach calls "valuing the moment." It involves thinking about what each element will feel like to the audience and how the next element can build on or bring closure to the emotion felt.

The value of direction became clear once again to me in a recent Program Development Meeting (PDM). My team and I were planning the last four-week series of the ministry season. We had chosen four very heavy topics: gangs, drugs, death, and sex. We asked ourselves these questions: "What do we want our students to feel?" And more important, "Where do we want our students to end up?" After tossing around several ideas, we decided to use a painful, real-life story each week that had a picture in the end of God's hope, healing, and strength.

Emotional direction can be determined by understanding your target's needs and the issues they are currently facing. For example, a local tragedy in your community may cause students to question God's goodness. If so, the direction your program takes could paint the picture of God's goodness even in the midst of sorrow or simply show the very real pain of loss. The key is to know your target well enough to respond to the circumstances surrounding them.

## Why Set Direction?

*"You use a glass mirror to see your face; you use a work of art to see your soul."*

GEORGE BERNARD SHAW [2]

Movie director Steven Spielberg knows how to move an audience emotionally. His award-winning movie *Schindler's List* evoked a spectrum of emotions—anger, joy, fear, and sadness—from people who viewed the movie. His dramatic portrayal showed the horrors of the Holocaust and the difference one man, Oskar Schindler, made in saving hundreds of Jews from death. The audience was moved not only through visual images, but also through powerful music. Spielberg chose a specific and powerful emotional direction to take. Many have chosen other emotional directions on the same historical event.

Another example of evoking powerful emotions was the recent movie *Braveheart*, with Mel Gibson playing the part of Scotsman William Wallace. Because Wallace was portrayed in this film as the Scottish "underdog," people who saw this movie probably began to feel emotions of passion and rage. As we watch a movie like this, we cheer for Wallace to conquer the English. But imagine if the story were told from the English perspective. Do you think you would feel the same emotions?

The emotional direction a movie, song, drama, video, or other artistic medium takes is important because it causes people to feel, sometimes to the very core of their soul. I am sure you can remember a specific movie, song, play, or book that touched you emotionally. What did you feel? Sadness? Happiness? Loneliness? Joy? Why did it affect you in such a meaningful way? Your soul might have been deeply touched, catching you by surprise and causing you to experience certain feelings for perhaps the first time.

Emotional direction in our programs is so important because the emotional tone can help our audience to be more open to spiritual matters. The direction your program takes has the potential to make your audience feel, maybe for the first time, in such a deep way that they open their hearts to the message of Christ. What a tremendous responsibility and opportunity!

A program that moves people towards spiritual change will help focus the choice of video, drama, Scripture reading, song, dance, to prepare the audience to hear the message. Wise use of the arts can begin to break down any walls a non-Christian may have put up and can soften his or her heart toward the truths of Christianity.

Don't misunderstand me. I am not suggesting that our efforts dictate God's presence or work in a program. But when you are intentional with the direction of the program, the arts can become a powerful tool to set up the message of Christ. Nancy Beach says this about Willow Creek's programming team's efforts:

> Our primary goal has been to use the arts to move the souls of people. We long to create moments that God can use to make people feel something deep down inside. Our Creator gave us music and all the other arts because He designed us to be emotive beings who respond to beauty and humor and celebration and tragedy.[3]

When you agree on the direction a program will take, you will avoid the pitfall of simply filling time slots and, instead, become more focused on building elements around the feeling you wish to evoke. There have been times when I and my programming team have reviewed a program and found that our direction wasn't clear and that it never helped the audience really feel anything. Sadly, we have missed many such opportunities over the years.

Direction can assist you in becoming more responsible with the time that you have in a program. Remember: You only have one shot, so make each minute count!

## How Do You Determine Direction?

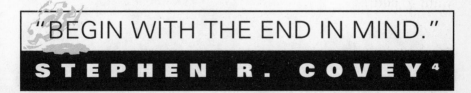

"BEGIN WITH THE END IN MIND."

STEPHEN R. COVEY[4]

Once you have developed a rationale statement, you are now ready to organize your first Program Development Meeting (PDM) to determine the program's direction. It is in this meeting that the program will start to take shape. Carefully think through who should attend this meeting. You want the right people in the room with you: people who walk authentically with Jesus Christ, who understand your ministry vision, and who are creative. Perhaps your whole programming team should be invited or maybe just a few key members. I have no magic number to suggest, except that when a group gets beyond twelve, it becomes difficult for each person's voice to be heard.

Over the years, we've developed a process at Student Impact that we find very effective in developing programs. Let me walk you through how we conduct a typical Program Development Meeting.

First, we hand out the rationale statement a few days before the meeting so that our team members can come prepared to brainstorm ideas. At the start of the meeting, we pray for God to give us His thoughts. Programming should never be based on our ideas, but on His. Our creativity comes from Him, and His ideas will never end.

After asking for God's direction, we write the rationale statement on a flip chart or dry-erase board. Next, right below the rationale, we write the topic we are presenting. Under both of those, we draw a large funnel that comes to the center of a target at the bottom of the page. At the bottom, next to the target, we write the answers to these two questions: "What do we want them to know?" and "What do we want them to do?"

Now we have a plan of where we would like the program to end up. The fun begins as we decide how we are going to get there. On one side of the funnel, we write down the felt need of our target, and on the other side we write down the spiritual truth we want to address.

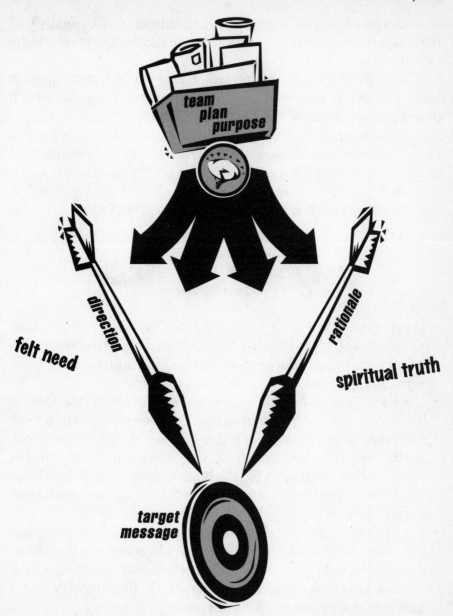

At this point we take some time to brainstorm all of the possible emotional directions the program could take. What are the students feeling? What emotions will help open their hearts to the truth presented in the message? When we have identified a number of possible directions, we evaluate which emotional direction could best set up a message and get us to our destination. We usually find that there is no right or wrong direction, though some may be more effective than others.

With the direction determined, we are ready to come up with ideas and begin planning the elements of the program. (We'll discuss this in detail in the next three chapters.)

Remember, the direction your program takes will paint a picture of God that will cause the audience to feel an emotion. That emotion will bring down some of the protective walls that guard their hearts. That breaking down of walls is what you need to shoot for as you determine your program's direction.

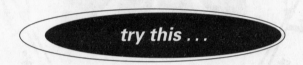

- Practice working with the funnel process on a few previous programs and try to improve them. This will give you some confidence and experience before leading a brainstorming team through this process.
- Use books, magazines, TV shows, and movies to look for possible directions to take on certain topics. Try to answer this question: "What is moving students today emotionally?" For example, *Surfing* magazine had a picture layout of some of the best places to surf called "Formulas for Excitement." We used this title for one of our recent series. And our "Real Friends" series title was a spin-off from the popular TV show *Friends*.
- In a brainstorming meeting, write a topic on flip-chart paper and ask your team to think of all the possible emotional directions a program could take. As you do this exercise, encourage team members to think "outside the box" and to come up with angles that may not be immediately obvious.
- If possible, take your team to a movie or a community theater production. Afterward, discuss how you feel and what emotions the movie or play evoked. Where did the movie or play take you emotionally? Which other roads of emotion could have been used?

## more resources

McDowell, Josh, and Bob Hostetler. *Josh McDowell's Handbook for Counseling Youth*. Dallas: Word, 1996.

Mueller, Walt. *Understanding Today's Youth Culture*. Wheaton, Ill.: Tyndale, 1994.

Olson, Dr. G. Keith. *Counseling Teenagers*. Loveland, Colo.: Group Books, 1984.

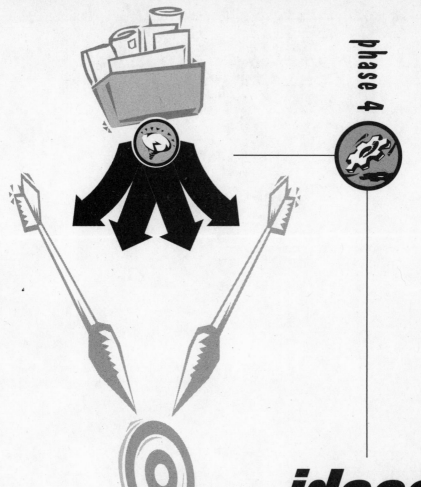

phase 4

ideas
resources
develop
produce

## See beyond the obvious

remember when I first saw those wild Magic Eye pictures in a store at a mall. These are the pictures that have dozens of colors and abstract shapes with images hidden within the picture. I was so intrigued with them, I decided to stop and try to find the secret images. A few people around me were also trying to discover the mysteries in the pictures.

As I stared for a few minutes at one of the pictures before me, I began to see elephants, giraffes, tigers, and eventually an entire jungle scene. I was not hallucinating—this image was real! I was amazed at what I could find. I went on to several other pictures and soon found James Dean, a baseball field, palm trees, and space scenes. Unfortunately, some of the people around me were not able to find the images. They tried and tried, but left the store frustrated.

Have you ever tried looking into those Magic Eye pictures? Did you see something or did they frustrate you? Could you look past the obvious, or did you feel left out, wondering if there was something wrong as others celebrated their new discoveries? Or perhaps you saw the pictures and just walked past them, thinking they were a waste of time.

Creative ideas are a lot like those pictures. For some, the hidden image is difficult to bring out, while for others—those who have the ability to see beyond the obvious—the hidden image seems to pop out effortlessly. You may not be an expert at seeing those Magic Eye pictures, but you *can* learn to see beyond the obvious and tap into your creative side when it comes to programming. We are all made in the image of the great Creator, and each of has been given, to some degree, a gift from heaven called creativity.

So far in the programming process, you have organized your plan, clarified its purpose, identified your target, refined your message, developed a rationale statement, and charted an emotional direction for the program. Now you are ready to begin to add color to your program with ideas that will help communicate the message of Jesus Christ in a creative way.

## What Is Creativity?

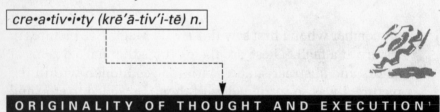

cre•a•tiv•i•ty (krē'ā-tiv'i-tē) n.

ORIGINALITY OF THOUGHT AND EXECUTION[1]

Every where we look, we see glimpses of God's limitless creativity. At the zoo, a zebra's stripes or a giraffe's long neck and brown polka dots reveal God's imagination and sense of humor. In my backyard, I marvel at the gracefulness of a deer and the beauty of an old oak tree. At the beach, the intricacy and delicacy of a sand dollar and the power of the crashing waves never cease to amaze me. When God created the world, He added color, beauty, and diversity to the land and sea, people, and animals.

Because He made us in His image, we, too, have been given the ability to be creative. He desires for us, as the body of Christ, to use creativity to take off the lid of status quo with new ideas that will paint an image of Him in our programs. Each one of us, even though our creativity may be at different levels, can contribute creativity to the team.

Albert Szent-Gyorgyi, the Nobel-prize-winning physician, summed up creativity when he said, "Discovery consists of looking at the same thing as everyone else and thinking something different."[2] That's the beauty of creativity; we each have our own unique perspective to bring to the team. We don't need magazines or movies, Hollywood directors, or New York marketing experts to hand us ideas. Charles "Chic" Thompson, founder of Creative Management Group, states:

> Creativity is not a trait monopolized by a few fortunate souls. Every person is creative, because creativity is the trait that makes us human.... To be creative is to have intelligence, to be able to gather information, and to make decisions based on that information. To be creative is to be able to perceive and recognize the world around us, to understand what we need or wish to do in response to it, and to set about changing it. To be creative is to find a way, a thought, an expression, a human manifestation no one else has found and to bring newly discovered possibilities into reality.[3]

Creative ideas can originate from unlikely sources and catch us by surprise. Consider several amazing ideas and what they developed into:

- Leo Gerstenzang thought of Q-tips when he saw his wife attempting to clean their baby's ears with toothpicks and cotton.
- Ole Evinrude got angry when the ice cream in his rowboat melted before he got to dry land, so he invented the outboard motor.
- Sylvan Goldman, the owner of two supermarket chains, noticed that customers rarely bought more items than they could carry in their arms. He "helped" shoppers carry more items to the check-out counter by inventing the shopping cart.
- Department store janitor Murray Spangler suffered discomfort from the dust his broom stirred up. He decided to suck up the dust instead and invented the vacuum cleaner.
- A waffle vendor came up with the idea for ice cream cones when he ran out of paper plates at the 1904 World's Fair in St. Louis.[4]

These ideas have changed the way we live. Can you imagine trying to clean your ears with toothpicks and cotton balls? In the same way, ideas can change the way our audience sees life and God. Don't believe the lie that you are not creative, for you have been created by God, the Master of creativity.

## Why Value Creativity?

> "The human mind once stretched to a new idea never goes back to its original dimensions."
>
> Oliver Wendell Holmes[5]

With so many great ideas all around us, why is it that we sometimes fall into a rut or seem content with doing programs the same way again and again? Creativity consultant Roger von Oech believes, "Most of us have certain attitudes that lock our thinking into the status quo and keep us thinking 'more of the same.' I call these attitudes mental locks."[6] Ten mental locks he warns against are:

1. The Right Answer
2. That's Not Logical
3. Follow the Rules
4. Be Practical
5. Play Is Frivolous
6. That's Not My Area
7. Avoid Ambiguity
8. Don't Be Foolish
9. To Err Is Wrong
10. I'm Not Creative

Have you and your team experienced any of these mental locks recently? von Oech suggests two ways to open these mental locks: temporarily unlearn them, or give yourself a whack on the side of the head to force yourself out of your routine. Perhaps some of us could use a "whack on the side of the head" in order to free us up to be more creative!

Ideas are critical to a company's success. Companies try continuously to sell new products or services. Many of these products are miraculously "new and improved," while others are gizmos or gadgets we are told we just can't live without. By generating ideas for new products, industries are able to transform themselves every couple of years.

Ideas can play an important part in our programs' effectiveness, too. God wants us to use the creativity He gave us to share His truth. He never said our programs had to be boring or predictable! Don't fall into a system of programming that shuts down new ideas. Instead, by using the arts and real-life stories, paint an image of God that your students can understand.

Generating and implementing new ideas will heighten your ability to relate to your target, especially as their culture is ever-changing. As speaker Ken Davis warns,

> Keeping up with the changes in our youth culture is not an easy task. But realize that ideas will always be there; they will never run out. We must be careful not to fall into the trap of believing that the methods that worked last year still will be effective in two years. Our audience will change. If we don't change with them, our message will not be heard.[7]

Creative ideas can increase your audience's desire to listen and to remember the truth being communicated. Creativity can be part of the catalyst that moves them toward spiritual life change.

A great idea that has created a lot of energy and become an effective element in our Sunday night Student Insight programs (our program for Christian students) has been our "Going Public" slot. Our ministry's Executive Director, Bo Boshers, came up with the idea to have students share personal stories of how God is changing their lives. To begin this part of the program, we play a song by the *Newsboys* called "Going Public." The Insight students respond with an eruption of cheering and applause when the student sharing his or her testimony gets to the stage and says, "Hi! My name is _____, and I am going public." It has become a significant part of our ministry on Sunday nights that we would have missed out on if we had not seen the value of a creative idea.

Christian leader Ted Engstrom states, "Creativity has been built into every one of us; it's part of our design. Each of us lives less of the life God intended for us when we choose not to live out the creative powers we possess."[8] Whether you are planning a large program or a small group meeting, using creative ideas to communicate the love of God pleases His heart.

## How Do You Stimulate Creativity?

*"Creativity is like a muscle—it has to be stretched and exercised regularly to keep it fit and functioning."*

GLORIA HOFFMAN AND PAULINE GRAIVIER[9]

If you sometimes feel that your ideas are about as creative as plain white bread, don't give up! You *can* become more creative—and bring out the best in the creative natures of your team, as well.

First, identify the times and places you feel most creative. We all have places that seem to spark our creativity. Dr. Yoshiro Nakamats, the inventor of the floppy disk, the compact disc, the compact disc player, and the digital watch, says he has a "special way of holding my breath and swimming underwater—that's when I come up with my best ideas. I've created a Plexiglas writing pad so that I can stay underwater and record these ideas. I call it 'creative swimming.'"[10] Hemingway found that he wrote best in cafes early in the morning. Duke Ellington wrote his music on trains. Descartes created his best ideas in bed. Edison slept in his lab so that whenever an idea came to him, he could write it down. Beethoven carried a notebook around with him so he could write down ideas for compositions wherever he was.[11] Just as most of us recognize our times of peak performance for other aspects of our work, so, too, we have places and times of day when we feel most creative.

For me, the mall, a bookstore, outdoors, or even a hardware store are places I go to get the idea ball rolling. One time when I was walking through a hardware store, I got ideas for a series we were about to do called "Takin' It to the Streets." I saw some chain link fence that I thought would look great behind the band and would give a "street" kind of feel to the stage. As I wondered about other ways to give the series title some visual impact, I thought of all the slogans that use the numeral 2 for the word "to." I bought some corrugated steel and used a blow torch to cut out the number

"2." We positioned a video screen behind it and showed footage of people on streets. A simple trip to the hardware store resulted in a dramatic backdrop that really set the tone for our series. Where are you when most of your creative ideas hit? Go there often!

Second, we are most creative when we are free from criticism or rejection and are willing to take risks. It is important to create an environment where no idea is a bad idea. That doesn't necessarily mean that every idea will be implemented, but no one should be put down for any suggestion. Michael Eisner, the chairman of Disney, is quoted as saying,

> At Disney, we also feel that the only way to succeed creatively is to fail. A company like ours must create an atmosphere in which people feel safe to fail. This means forming an organization where failure is not only tolerated, but fear of criticism for submitting a foolish idea is abolished. If not, people become too cautious. They hunker down ... afraid to speak up, afraid to rock the boat, afraid of being ridiculed. Potentially brilliant ideas are never uttered ... and therefore never heard.[12]

As Christians, we have an advantage that Disney does not: they are standing behind a mouse, but we have the God of the Universe on our side. His Holy Spirit will lead us if only we will slow down enough to listen. His ideas are never bad ideas. We must create an atmosphere among the team that welcomes ideas from all members.

Nancy Beach contends, "Powerful church services result primarily from the voice of God giving ideas and inspiration to undeserving people like you and me.... God still speaks to those who listen. He is and always will be the Ultimate Creator—and I have learned that His storehouse will never grow empty of wonderful ideas."[13] We must discipline ourselves to listen and then present our ideas with confidence, knowing that God is the inspiration behind them.

The third way to stimulate creativity is to brainstorm. In the "Try This" section, I have listed a few brainstorming techniques. According to creativity expert Roger von Oech, there are two main phases in the development of new ideas: the imaginative phase and the practical phase. "In the imaginative phase, you generate and play with ideas.... The motto of the imaginative phase is: Thinking something different. . . . In the practical phase, you evaluate and execute them [the ideas]. . . . The motto of the practical phase is: Getting something done."[14] Brainstorming sessions work so well because they create an environment of imagination, excitement, and at some point, a reality check. I have found four ways that ensure brainstorming sessions are as productive as possible.

First, begin by assembling the right people. You need to select about ten to fifteen people who have some understanding of your program's target. There are basically two types of people when it comes to ideas: Idea Starters and Idea Followers. Idea Starters are those people who can generate ideas in a moment's notice; ideas seem to come easily to them. Idea Followers are just as important. While Idea Followers need to be well into the brainstorming process in order for their creative juices to flow, they usually offer a "golden nugget" idea if you are patient enough to wait.

Once you've determined what people you need on your brainstorming team, the second thing to do is to create the optimal environment. Take some time to prepare the meeting room. Make sure there is plenty of paper to write on; storyboarding materials if you can get them; a selection of current magazines, Bibles, and books; and a large table so that everyone has a place to write. Food also helps bring out creativity! The environment can either make or break your session time, so make it comfortable and interesting. Our church's programming team has a box of Frisbees and Nerf toys in the room to help break any tension or creativity blocks.

Third, as your team works, lead by cheerleading. Your job is to make sure everyone feels cheered for and spurred on with the ideas they contribute. Your encouragement will set the tone so that each team member can feel safe offering ideas. The moment someone in the room dominates or becomes critical, the creative chemistry of the group is at risk.

Finally, don't force ideas. Ideas can be very finicky. If they aren't coming, then don't be afraid to move on. Ask God to infuse you and your team to work together creatively. He will provide the right ideas at just the right time.

As you brainstorm ideas for music, art, and video, keep in mind copyright laws. Most movies available on video are licensed for home viewing only. If you want to show a clip in your program, you need to get permission. Most Christian music companies allow you to make slides so you can project the words to songs, but you do need to get their permission first to be within legal and ethical guidelines. You will find the names of some movie and music licensing organizations listed in the "More Resources" section at the end of this chapter.

As my team brainstormed for the "Real Friends" series, we came up with many great ideas. Here are some of the ideas we thought of for the program titled "Real Friends Stay."

- Movie clips showing classic scenes of friends
- Friendship songs:
    "Friends" by Michael W. Smith
    "You've Got a Friend" by James Taylor
    "Don't Speak" by No Doubt
    "Desperado" by the Eagles
    "Let's Stand Together" by The Kry
    "All Kinds of People" by Susan Ashton
- A sad story of a friend losing a friend
- Reading letters (live or on video) to best friends
- Drama:
    A student monologue of someone who is bitter over losing a friend
    Showing the positive side of someone sticking with a friend through a hard time
- Video ideas:
    On-the-street interviews: "Who is your best friend and why?"
    Videotape a friends' night out (like the TV show *A Real World*)
    Multimedia scenes of different friends, set to the theme song of the TV show *Friends*
- Live interview of two friends talking about their friendship

In chapter 10 you'll see which ideas we ultimately chose and how we put them together into a program.

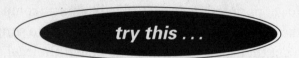

*try this . . .*

- Get away from the TV! Television is the single worst creativity killer today. If you often find yourself sitting in front of the television during your free time, try reading a book instead.
- One brainstorming method is called "storyboarding." Team members write down their ideas for a particular topic on index cards and place them on a large bulletin board, called a story-board, according to elements suggested, like music or video. This technique allows everyone to participate and usually gives you plenty of ideas from which to choose.
- Another effective brainstorming method is to write a topic in the middle of a dry-erase board or piece of flip-chart paper and draw a circle around it. Then list all the possible ideas related to this topic around the outside of the circle.
- Walk through a mall and write down everything that gives you an idea.
- Go to a bookstore and look at what is on the shelves.
- Go to a music store and listen to music you wouldn't normally listen to.
- Keep an idea notebook with you all the time and build an idea file you can refer to regularly.
- Search the Internet for any material related to your topic.
- Interview someone in your target audience.
- Reuse great ideas. Everybody does!
- Attend the theater in your city or the local college theater. You can get great ideas for themes, staging, and music.

*more resources*

DeBono, Edward. *Serious Creativity*. New York: Harper Business, 1992.
_____. *Six Thinking Hats*. New York: Little, Brown & Company, 1986.
Firestien, Roger L. *Leading on the Creative Edge*. Colorado Springs: Pinon Press, 1996.

von Oech, Roger. *A Kick in the Seat of the Pants*. New York: Harper & Row, 1986.

_____. *A Whack on the Side of the Head*. New York: Warner Books Inc., 1990.

_____. *Creative Whack Pack*. Stamford, Connecticut: US Games Systems Inc., 1992.

Dyer, Scott and Nancy Beach. *The Source*. Grand Rapids: Zondervan, 1996.

Thompson, Charles "Chic." *What a Great Idea*. New York: Harper Perennial, 1992.

## Music Copyright Licensing

ASCAP (American Society of Composers, Authors, and Publishers): 1–800–505–4052.

BMI (Broadcast Music, Incorporated): For licensing information call 1–800–925–8451; for general queries call 1–800–800–9313.

CCLI (Christian Copyright Licensing International): 1–800–234–2446.

## Movie Copyright Licensing

Films, Inc.: 1–800–323–4222.

MPLC (Motion Picture Licensing Corporation): 1–800–462–8855.

Swank Motion Pictures: 1–800–876–3330.

# Step 9

# resources

## One person's trash could be another's treasure

Fighter pilot Scott O'Grady had trained for months to learn how to handle all kinds of potential emergencies. It was a good thing he was prepared. When his F-16 was cut in half by a Bosnian missile four miles above enemy territory, O'Grady ejected from the cockpit and pulled the rip cord of his parachute. As he descended to earth, he knew he had to think fast, because Serbian soldiers would immediately be looking for him. When he landed, he ran into the woods and put his face in the dirt. O'Grady was afraid that the white of his skin would stand out, so he covered his head and ears with his flying gloves.

He lay motionless for five hours as soldiers passed by just a few feet away. Later that evening, O'Grady finished the water in his survival gear and began to pray for rain. God answered his prayer with a torrential downpour. O'Grady used a sponge to soak up water from the ground and his clothes and also wrung out his soggy socks for drinking water.

Fortunately, O'Grady had with him an evasion chart, a three-foot-by-five-foot waterproof sheet, which he used to keep himself warm at night. When hunger pangs hit, O'Grady ate ants and grass. At night, O'Grady began signaling from his handheld radio. A rescue mission was organized. On the morning of the sixth day, O'Grady's yellow flare was spotted by the Air Force and O'Grady was rescued.

Scott O'Grady survived for six days in the woods by being resourceful. He used his survival pack and what was around him to endure until help arrived. We, too, can not only survive but thrive in our ministries by using what we already have and also by looking for the potential resources around us. By the time you arrive at this step in program development, you have brainstormed some great ideas and are probably wondering how to implement them. Resources are the means to pull off your ideas and make them become reality.

Fortune 500-sized budgets and creative geniuses are not necessary to plan purposeful and innovative programs. You just need to be wise with the resources you do have and persistent in finding new ones. Learning how to search for resources will take a burden off of your budget, remind you to trust God to provide, and also encourage those on your programming team to be resource-conscious.

## What Are Resources?

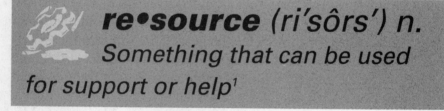

**re•source** *(ri'sôrs') n.*
*Something that can be used for support or help*[1]

Tricia and I are suckers for a good garage sale. It's not just the prices that are attractive; garage sales are graveyards of hidden treasures. People will get rid of anything that does not have perceived value to them.

Most of the furniture and decorations in our home are someone's garage sale junk. We once found a beat-up old desk that had apparently reached its functional end to the seller but to us appeared valuable. We knew we could refinish and repair it, so we bought it for twenty-five dollars and spent another twenty-five repairing and refinishing it. The antique oak missionary desk is now worth much more and sits in our living room as a morning altar for us to be with our Lord. The desk was someone's trash, but now it is our treasure.

Ministry resources go beyond tangible finds at garage sales, but the same principle applies: finding treasures in "trash" can bring your program ideas to life.

In ministry and specifically for programs, resources are the network of people, printed materials, and equipment that can support and help meet your programming needs. Notice that the above definition of *resource* uses the word *support*. Resources *support* programs, but they do not *make* them. The greatest lights or the best sound board will prove meaningless if programs are not purposeful in painting an image of God. On the flip side, a purposeful program carried out with minimal financial resources can still be tremendously effective in reaching students for Christ. Whether we have a small programming budget or a large one, all of us can creatively use resources to support and help our programs.

Recently, a high school student minister called me and expressed discouragement that his ministry could not afford to purchase equipment or pay someone to edit videos for his ministry's weekly programs. I asked him if there were any small colleges in his area. He knew of two. I challenged him to find out if these colleges had video departments. If so, perhaps a Christian who was a communications major would be interested in serving; he or she would benefit from the hands-on ministry experience. I also told him that these colleges might rent equipment or let their majors use the equipment. Together, we had hit upon a resource "gold mine"! Not only did this student minister find someone who could edit videos, but he also found a person willing to offer his gifts to serve Christ in the church—another servant for his programming team!

Sometimes the resources around us are not always obvious. I once saw a program that had used orange construction fencing as a stage backdrop with some lights. It looked great! Who would have ever thought construction materials could be potential treasures for a program? Perhaps you have some carpenters in your congregation who could provide scrap materials as part of a set for an upcoming program. Whether it's a mom who loves to write and could create drama scripts, or a corporate executive who has a graphics department that could design flyers and logos, building a network of people who are willing to help you meet ministry needs is important. People are a valuable resource.

Many excellent printed materials can also be valuable resources to you and your ministry. Just as I hope this book is a helpful resource for you, others involved in student ministry can contribute to your programming team through what they write and publish. Group Books, Zondervan Publishing House, and Youth Specialties offer numerous books, small group curricula, and programming ideas to those serving in student ministry. (Note their phone numbers in the "More Resources" section at the end of this chapter so that you may order a product catalog.) Student Impact now offers small group curricula manuals, a book on conducting competitions, a camps and retreats book, and a book on student ministry philosophy and strategy, all published by Zondervan. With all published materials, be wary of the temptation to use a "packaged program" without evaluating it in light of your ministry purpose. Remember: Resources support the program; they do not make the program.

Equipment is another crucial resource. Whether big or small, cheap or expensive, new or used, equipment assists in developing programs. Too often, people in ministry get frustrated because they feel they lack the budget for proper equipment. Even though it can be challenging to work with limited funds, it cannot become an excuse to be dull and uncreative in our programs. I once heard excellence being referred to as doing the best with what you have. Whether you have a lot or a little, you can create excellent and exciting programs by searching for the resources around you.

## Why Find Resources?

*"One of the major factors which differentiates creative people from lesser creative people is that creative people pay attention to their small ideas."*

**ROGER VON OECH**[2]

I have always been fascinated by the creativity in the motion pictures industry. I enjoy seeing a movie with a new digital or special effect. Movies seem to get better and more creative every year. *Star Wars* was re-released twenty years after it first hit the theaters because George Lucas found new ways to enhance the original movie with innovative special effects. He was not content with the status quo even though the movie had been immensely popular in its time. He knew he could make it better.

Our attitude in ministry should be like George Lucas'. We should strive to find ways to "do" our programs better and to improve them with resources. If we truly believe that resources support the program and the message we want to communicate, we will want to build that support into everything we do. We cannot be lazy and think that, just because it's church, we can be satisfied with "getting by."

Without resources, ideas would simply stay just ideas. People and materials are needed to bring them to life. Finding and using resources by networking time, talents, and treasures will bear more fruit than any Hollywood budget ever could.

Needing resources will also convey to your church and team members that you need them. Those who share resources and help you find them will know they are an important part of your ministry. It really is just another way the church was meant to function together.

## How Do You Find Resources?

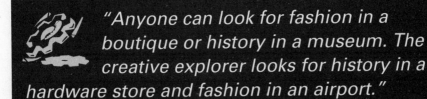

*"Anyone can look for fashion in a boutique or history in a museum. The creative explorer looks for history in a hardware store and fashion in an airport."*

Robert Wieder[3]

It's a known fact that most trees have roots in the ground at least twice as deep as the tree is tall. The rule of thumb I like to use in finding resources is to develop a network of resources twice as big as the immediate need. By this, I mean to build a resource list that is full of potential opportunities. Even though you don't see a need for a particular resource at the moment, you may need it for a future program, so save it. Every time you connect with a resource, you deepen your resource roots.

The best way to start deepening your roots is by talking to the people around you—in your neighborhood, your church, the health club, your children's school, etc.—and getting to know what they do professionally and what kinds of hobbies they have. Start a file with names and numbers so that when a need arises for your program, you have a starting place to look. As your needs increase and your network grows, you will find your ideas are much easier to pull off and also less expensive.

People will donate their resources more often to ministries they believe in. One of our ministry parent volunteers, for example, owns a print shop and will always cut us a break on printing. One of our most helpful computer resources was a student who could write databases, repair hardware and software, and train our staff. And sometimes people less connected to your ministry will be willing to make a donation for tax purposes. One warning, however: Don't let yourself fall into the trap of valuing people only for what they can do for you or for your ministry!

Networking with people is one of the best resources for your ministry. In Student Impact, we have formed AIM, which stands for Associated Impact Ministries. AIM is a group of like-minded men and women who provide one another with support, encouragement, and networking. Some of the leaders from this group have traded equipment, shared messages and drama scripts, and swapped programming ideas. If you would like more information on how to be a part of AIM, please see the "More Resources" section at the end of this chapter.

Another way I deepen my resource roots is, believe it or not, junk mail. Before you throw out the many catalogs you receive, take a look. I keep a file of catalogs in my office and refer to them quite often. Catalogs that include trinkets, sports catalogs, clothing, and graphics are all great places to start resourcing.

Not only do I use catalogs as a resource, I am also always on the lookout for new published resources, like books, manuals, music, and videos. The criteria for what gets filed is that it must have practical value to my target audience now or possibly in the future. And it must be something that can be used or be helpful in creating a better program.

As you deepen your resource roots, don't forget to communicate your programming needs, whether it be a need for more people on your team or a need for equipment. Put an announcement in your church bulletin. Post a flyer on the local college or community center bulletin board. And just keep looking and talking to people!

*try this . . .*

- List all the colleges and technical schools in your area that could be potential "fishing ponds." At each school, look for graphic artists, musicians, speech majors, video related majors, etc., by talking with professors or putting flyers on bulletin boards discribing your ministry and your programming needs.
- Start building a resource file of catalogs, books, music, and videos. Be sure to create a filing system that is organized enough for you to find information when you need it. If the information is unorganized, you will simply build a file cabinet full of paper!
- Never pass up a good garage sale. You might be surprised what you find!
- Develop a list of people you know who could offer possible special resources in the future. Even if you don't see what use their resource has right now, you may need it at a later date.
- Identify the production, stage, video, and multimedia businesses in your area. If possible, visit a few of these companies and try to make connections.
- Make an inventory list of what equipment your ministry has: cameras, instruments, computers, etc. Ask your programming team members what kind of equipment they own and might be willing to share.
- Go through your entire church and make an inventory list of everything in storage (paint, paint supplies, props, equipment, paper, pens, old clothes, raw materials, signs, Bibles, etc.). This way you'll know what is already on hand.

- Take advantage of the Internet. Learn how to use it by reading manuals or books so that you can search it for resources and ideas.

## Multimedia

AIM (Associated Impact Ministries): For more information, call the Willow Creek Association at (847) 765–0070 or write to P.O. Box 3188, Barrington, IL 60010.

Edge TV: 1–800–616-EDGE. Each video contains a variety of segments on different issues you can use to stimulate discussion.

interl'inc: 1–800–725–3300. This organization links people and resources in the Christian music industry with student ministries. Subscribers receive the hottest nine contemporary Christian albums, the best Christian music videos, and Bible studies relating to the themes of the music. Call for more information about how interl'inc can assist your ministry.

Internet: The Willow Creek Association has a web page at www.willowcreek.org. At this writing, Student Impact's web page, WIN City, has an idea factory, a resource museum, a news house, and a network village. Check the Willow Creek Association web page for a link.

Microsoft Cinemania CD ROM: A reference library of movies, organized by title, topic, director, star, etc. Available in computer stores.

Microsoft Music Central CD ROM: A reference library of music, organized by title, topic, artist, etc. Available in computer stores.

The Shepherd's Guide: A phone directory of Christian-owned businesses. Call the Chicago office at (847) 265–0020 for information about your area.

## Publishers

Group Books: 1–800–447–1070
Willow Creek Resources: 1–800–876–7335
Youth Specialties: 1–800–776–8008
Zondervan Publishing House: 1–800–727–1309

# Step 10

# *develop*

## Treasures take time

When an irritant, like a grain of sand, becomes trapped inside an oyster's shell, an amazing wonder of nature begins to develop. Over time, the dirty sand becomes a prized treasure, a pearl. Humans have discovered a way to cultivate pearls by manually placing an irritant into a living oyster and then letting it develop over time. Shallow water speeds growth, but deeper, cooler water improves the quality of the pearls. Pearls may be harvested as soon as five years after implantation, but longer periods of cultivation produce a finer product.[1] It takes hard work and time to produce precious pearls.

Our programs, too, need time to develop into Spirit-led treasures. After you have determined direction, brainstormed ideas, and located resources, you are now ready to organize all the elements, from props to people, to produce a program that radiates the life-changing message of Jesus Christ.

## What Does It Mean to Develop?

de•vel•op (dē-vel'ep)
v. To improve the quality of; refine[2]

Improving and refining is exactly what we are trying to do as we develop our programs. We want the ideas we have brainstormed to come together into a clear presentation of Jesus Christ. Ideally, we have many ideas to choose from. Most likely, we will need to make adjustments, both big and small, to our ideas and figure out the most effective way for them to be used in our programs. This takes time and hard work.

Developing a program begins in the Program Development Meeting (PDM). As I mentioned earlier, at Student Impact the PDM is a weekly scheduled meeting where the programming team reviews a program's rationale, brainstorms ideas, and develops those ideas into an order for the program. When a program order is being developed in PDM, elements like music, video, drama, or a testimony are moved around, reviewed, and refined. Each person and element is looked at to determine where it might fit best in the program based on the direction that program is headed. Never casually throw elements or people together merely to fill slots and hope for the best. Instead, make sure there is a purpose for each person and element in the program's order.

Start by looking at your blank canvas as you combine creative and purposeful elements in hopes of painting an image of God. Sometimes your team will create a "masterpiece" fairly quickly and the elements will seem to just fall into place. Usually, though, you will need to get the paint out again and again and attempt to paint a clearer image. Just as fine wine goes through a fermenting process, so, too, ideas need time to ferment and be refined. You may need to tweak an idea or throw it out and start over.

Here, for example, is the program order for week four of our "Real Friends" series:

8:00  Walk-in: Contemporary Christian music on CD
8:05  Song: "You've Got a Friend in Me" by Randy Newman

8:10 Video: Copyright-approved clip from a popular movie depicting friends sticking together

8:12 Verbal: Series review. Jarrett Stevens (ministry staff member) gives an overview of what has been learned and introduces the next song

8:16 Song: "Don't Speak" by No Doubt, performed by Stephanie (member of the vocal team)

8:20 Video: "Best Friends IV," a video showing Melissa, a student, talking about her best friend

8:21 Verbal: Topic introduction: Melissa tells a story about her friend sticking by her

8:24 Song: "You've Got a Friend" by James Taylor, performed by Nate (member of the vocal team)

8:28 Transition: Guitar reprise

8:30 Drama: "Real Friends?" A dramatic monologue of a girl who is bitter because she has no real friends in the tough times

8:35 Video: "A Real Friend Is. . . ." Students from different high schools describing what they see as the qualities of a real friend

8:37 Message: "Real Friends Stay." Bo Boshers helps students know the only Real Friend, Jesus Christ

8:57 Verbal: Announcements regarding upcoming ministry events

9:00 Walk-out: A collection of contemporary Christian songs about friends

This program was developed over weeks of brainstorming and planning. We were pleased that, in a purposeful, effective way, it helped students learn about friendship with God.

## Why Develop?

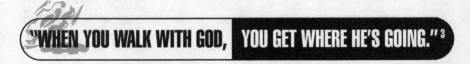

"WHEN YOU WALK WITH GOD, YOU GET WHERE HE'S GOING."[3]

Suppose you could have the entire world, every person living on the planet, as your audience for one single program to communicate the gospel message. You would have no second service, no next week—just one program. Wouldn't you want to ensure the best possible effort was made to communicate this most important message? What would you do? Would you strive to develop each element so that it fit perfectly? Would you prepare each person on stage with what they were to say or do? How seriously would you take each planning session? I'm sure you would spend hours planning, refining, and practicing for such a big program.

This illustration is not too far-fetched. While we do not have the whole world as our captive audience, God has entrusted students to our ministry who desperately need to hear that the free gift of salvation is available to them if they will believe. We may only have one chance to communicate this message to the small world of students in our midst. We need to spend the time and work necessary to present the very best we have in each program opportunity in our ministries.

Creating an excellent program requires that we develop the program as well as the personnel. Let's take a closer look at each of these areas.

## How Do You Develop Programs and Personnel?

> ### "A structured process for creativity helps you to work the problem more efficiently."
>
> ROGER L. FIRESTIEN[4]

One of the most effective tools I have found to develop a program is through use of the funnel, which we briefly discussed in chapter 7.

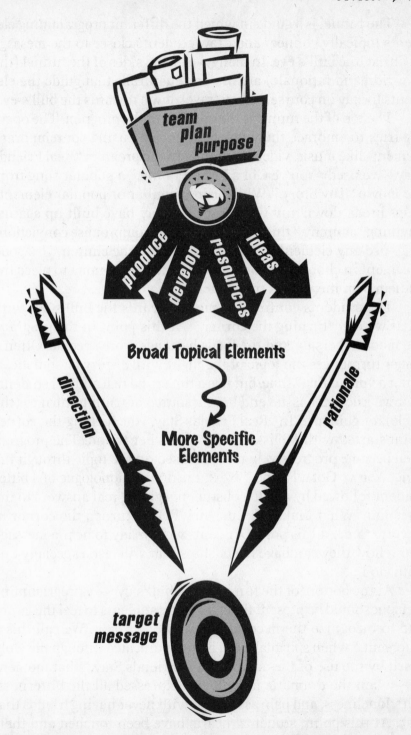

The funnel is a guide in which the different programming elements topically connect and draw students closer to the message of Christ, the bull's-eye. In many ways, the sides of the funnel (the direction and rationale) are like the guardrails that guide the elements to stay on course as they travel down towards the bull's-eye.

The top of the funnel is the opening of the program. The opening tries to embrace the whole audience by using contemporary elements like music, video, or drama. In the program "Real Friends Stay," we used "You've Got a Friend in Me," a popular song from the movie "Toy Story." While using familiar or popular elements helps break down any walls a seeker may have built up against anything "churchy," this is not a license to compromise convictions or to use any element that isn't edifying to the church. Use good judgment in choosing a popular song, video, or drama to place the audience on the topical train tracks.

The students continue to move towards the bull's-eye with what we call "turning the corner." At this point in the program, the mood sobers up and the focus becomes more specific. Often a leader introduces the topic of the night with a story or statistic. It is not a "preaching" time, but it is a time to be real and tell students that we know the issue and have a source of truth to turn to (the Bible) for guidance. In "Real Friends Stay," the turning-the-corner point started with Melissa's story about her friend. The program then became progressively more focused on the topic through the song "You've Got a Friend." Next, the drama monologue of a bitter student followed by a video of students giving real answers to the question "What Makes Friendships Real?" turned the corner in the program. At this point, students were ready to hear a message about how they can have friendships that will last, especially one with God.

At the bottom of the funnel—the bull's-eye—a programming element should be present that will cause students to feel the issues and to recognize the need for an answer or help. We call this a "moment," when spiritual truth is communicated through the Holy Spirit by the use of the arts. In "Real Friends Stay," that moment was when the dramatic monologue expressed all the bitterness, hurt, loneliness, and pain associated with never having friends that stay. At this point, students' hearts have been touched and their minds are ready to hear the message of truth.

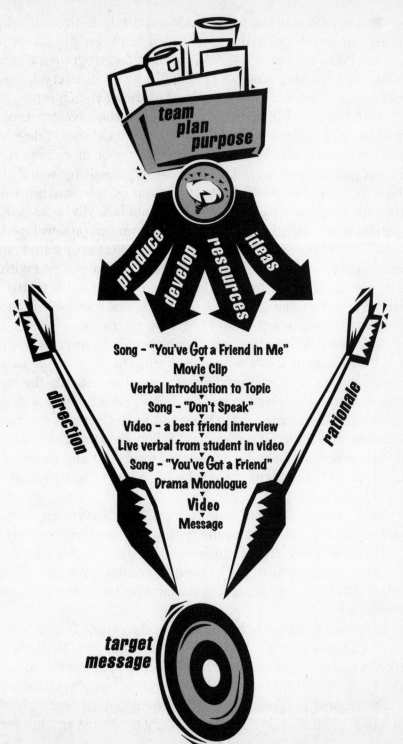

team
plan
purpose

produce
develop
resources
ideas

direction

rationale

Song – "You've Got a Friend in Me"
Movie Clip
Verbal Introduction to Topic
Song – "Don't Speak"
Video – a best friend interview
Live verbal from student in video
Song – "You've Got a Friend"
Drama Monologue
Video
Message

target
message

At every stage in the funnel, it is important to think through details. For instance, using transitions between programming elements helps to weave a thread through the program and keep it connected. To keep track of the details, we write every element on a cue sheet, which we'll talk about in the next chapter.

While using a funnel helps to develop a cohesive program, it would be in vain if we neglected the more critical side of development: developing people. People should always be more important than programs. At Student Impact, we try hard to uphold this value. We want our ministry to be driven by relationships, not programs. Program-driven ministry will not last. God uses people to do His work, and through them a program can be developed.

Whether they are adults or students, musicians or sound engineers, people involved in the program need to be developed within a safe setting so that they will mature into humble servants of Christ. We want them to develop their gifts and talents, but, more important, we challenge them to develop their souls.

As leaders, we need to invest in the people on our teams. This kind of investment starts with identifying the players and determining who the "hitters" are. Hitters are not necessarily the most gifted or the best-looking members, but those who have a desire to use a gift, are humble, and in love with Jesus Christ. A great way to find out who these players are is to follow the Holy Spirit's leading. Ask yourself: "Who brings energy to my life and ministry?" "In whom do I see potential?" "Who has a visibly authentic walk with Jesus Christ?"

Next, you must give these players opportunities to hit the ball. You must give them chances that will help them improve, yet in which they feel safe enough to fail. Allow the hitters a chance to take more responsibility in the program and to own something. During this time, you become a coach who helps them develop their skills.

Last, you must be a cheerleader. Make people feel as if they have the most supportive fan spurring them on: you. Never forget the power of an encouraging word or a comforting note. You can make a difference in their lives. Encourage, encourage, encourage!

Developing programs and personnel is not an exact science. You will get better at developing by doing programs and honestly evaluating both the process and the end result. Developing takes purposeful effort and some grace as you make mistakes, but when you begin to develop programs and the people on your team, you open a door for the ministry of God to work in the lives of students. Are you ready to open that door?

- Ask your team how they feel about the upcoming program and if they have any suggestions or additional ideas to improve it.
- Review each program order, no matter how sound it may seem, to see if there is a more effective order. This will stimulate the team's thinking and test the strength of what you already have.
- Appoint a few people on your team to play "devil's advocate" and try to find any holes in your program order.
- As you select and order the program elements, listen to the full songs, videos, and drama scripts so you can "feel" the flow.
- Bring in a person from your target audience to give you some "feed-up" on the program order. ("Feed-up" is giving your opinion before the event happens, rather than afterwards, which is "feed-back.")
- Make it a weekly goal to develop those on your team in some way. Consider these possibilities:

    Allow team members to own a part of the program. For example, let the vocalists sing, the actors act, etc.

    Write a note encouraging a team member's authentic walk with Christ or affirming how God used that person's unique gift in a recent program.

    **Caution:** In programming, it is tempting to buy into talent. We call it the "hired gun" trap. A person may have an incredible voice or be able to act, but if he or she is not in love with Jesus or has serious ego problems, we run the risk of diluting the message we are trying to communicate. Remember that the people on your stage communicate a stronger message with who they are than with what they say or do. Protect the stage by knowing the hearts of those who are on it.

**more resources**

Blanchard, Kenneth. *The One Minute Manager Builds High Performing Teams.* New York: William Morrow and Company, Inc., 1990.

Covey, Stephen R. *Principle-Centered Leadership.* New York: Summit Books, 1990.

Hybels, Bill. *Building Bigger Hearts* tape series. Call Seeds at 1–800–570–9812 to order.

Maxwell, John C. *Developing the Leaders Around You.* Nashville: Nelson, 1995.

# Step produce

## See the big picture

ark is confused and sad because his parents' twenty-year marriage recently came to a screeching halt. He questions God and is angry that this has happened to his family. He needs to hear about the love of God.

Katie grew up in a Christian home and is growing as a believer. It's her senior year and she is trying to make some big decisions—should she go a Christian college or a state school, and should she keep dating Joe, her boyfriend of three years. She's really searching for God's direction, but could use some biblical teaching and encouragement.

Brian is a freshman who just wants to fit in. His new high school friends are pressuring him to join a gang, but Brian keeps putting them off. He knows in his heart that it would be a bad decision to join, but he is unsure of where else to look for acceptance. Brian needs to hear that God accepts him and can provide hope for his life.

Sarah is in love, or at least she thinks she is. She is a Christian, but sees no problem in dating Ryan, who is not a believer. Lately, Ryan has been pressuring her to have sex. Sarah does not know what to do; if they are in love, isn't sex okay? Sarah needs to hear of God's unconditional love and His guidelines for relationships.

Kurt is a sophomore who works two part-time jobs. His father is out of work and is an alcoholic. His mom is tired from taking care of his brother and sister every day and then heading off to her evening job. Kurt has tried church, but doesn't feel God cares about his situation. He needs to see how much God loves him and realize that the gift of salvation is available to him.

Imagine that these students came to your ministry, each of them empty in some way and looking for answers. In different ways, each student is seeking God. Our programs must address students' needs and provide the answers for which they are searching. We should feel the responsibility to be purposeful with every minute of every program done in our ministries so that students will understand the love of God.

After you have worked through the programming process discussed in this book, your program is ready for production. All your efforts and prayers have come together at one place and time for one purpose. All the meetings, planning, administration, creating, and brainstorming have come together for this one program. You think to yourself about how it will be received. Your excitement level grows as you mentally run through everything that must happen in order for the program to be successful. You are without a doubt ready, but you still sense the program could be sharpened if only you could see it.

If you are like me, you love these days! Tension is high because you know that the stakes are high, but it never outweighs the excitement for kingdom impact. I always want to remember that there are Marks, Katies, Brians, Sarahs, and Kurts out in the audience, each hoping that the program will provide an answer for their searching souls. Eternity hangs in the balance.

This step in the program development process is where all the elements line up and the program is ready to roll. Every step of the process thus far was necessary for you to even be at this place. With all the steps up to this point in the process completed, you can confidently present the program. You are ready to produce.

## What Does It Mean to Produce?

pro•duce (pre-dōōs') v.

*To bring forward; to offer to view or notice[1]*

I was twenty-one years old and sitting in a hot locker room with fifty of my football teammates late one Saturday afternoon. We were all taped, dressed in brand new bowl jerseys, and prepared to take the field. We had been in this place more times than I could count. The difference, though, for me and about half the guys in the locker room, was that this would be the last competitive football game we ever played. This realization hit me hard! I thought about all the training, pain, coaching, injuries, learning, and experiences I had accumulated in seven years of playing football. Tonight had to be my best performance ever. All that I had become from those years of training needed to show up on the field. I needed to produce. My teammates felt it too. It wasn't something our coaches said; all of us knew what we had to do. We took the field that night and played one of the most inspirational games I have ever seen to beat the country's toughest junior college. We produced, and won the game!

For you, your "game day" experience may be a test, a challenge at work, or a last day at something. When you think about that experience, can you remember how you wanted to make a statement, a lasting impression on those around you? You wanted everything you had become to surface at that moment.

Producing a program is much like that "game day" experience. You pull from everything you and your team have learned and prepared for during one program. You offer the product of all that your teams have planned, prayed, brainstormed, and rehearsed for. You want to produce a lasting impression that will change lives.

Every year at Student Impact, we plan, develop, and produce more than one hundred different programs, ranging in time, topic, and target. The moment we forget the "game day" attitude about any program, we set ourselves up for disappointment or failure.

## Why Produce?

"GOD HOLDS US RESPONSIBLE, NOT FOR WHAT *we have,* BUT FOR WHAT *we could have;* NOT FOR WHAT *we are,* BUT FOR WHAT *we might be.*"[2]

If you had asked me in the locker room after my last football game, "Why were you trying harder than ever to make an impact?" my answer would have been, "Because today was the last chance I would ever have to play football!" I wanted to go out having the best game of my career.

When asked the question, "Why take the time to produce a program?" the answer is obvious to me: it might very well be the last opportunity I have to present to someone in the audience the life-changing message of Jesus Christ. We produce because it is a part of giving our best. It helps organize and orchestrate a team of efforts into one program that is purposeful and clear and paints an image of God.

You might ask, "Why the urgency?" As our society continues to deteriorate morally and family units keep collapsing, this is what the Marks, Katies, Brians, Sarahs, and Kurts are facing every day in America:

- 1,000 unwed teenage girls become mothers;
- 1,106 teenage girls get abortions;
- 4,219 teenagers contract sexually transmitted diseases;
- 500 adolescents begin using drugs;
- 1,000 adolescents begin drinking alcohol;

- 135,000 kids bring guns or other weapons to school;
- 3,610 teens are assaulted; 80 are raped;
- 2,200 teens drop out of high school;
- 6 teens commit suicide.[3]

Shouldn't these statistics be reason enough for us as leaders in ministry to face the programming challenge as if it were game day?

The good news is that we have the answer students are looking for: a relationship with Jesus Christ. We produce programs because we want students to hear about the love of Jesus Christ and then choose to become fully devoted followers of Him. Our desire is that the programs we produce be used by God to affect life change in students.

## How Do You Produce?

"BE AWARE OF EVERYTHING THAT IS GOING ON AROUND YOU— UP, DOWN, BEHIND YOU, ALL OVER. LISTEN NOT ONLY TO WHAT IS SAID, BUT ALSO TO WHAT IS NOT SAID. NOTICE WHAT IS DONE AND WHAT IS NOT DONE. INSIGHTS COME FROM WHAT IS NOT SAID AND WHAT IS NOT DONE."

CAROL ANDERSON[4]

I have often been inspired by the work of artists, coaches, and professionals who move and empower teams to produce something. One of those experiences was during the summer after my high school graduation. I had attended my best friend, Mike Marcums's, Marine Corps Boot Camp Graduation in San Diego. I'll never forget seeing several hundred men marching in perfect step. Every move of every arm and leg was in unison. It was an incredible sight. In front of every one of the several platoons was a leader—a drill instructor—barking out simple yet very exact commands that his men responded to immediately. No second guessing. No confusion. Only an immediate response. It was a powerful picture of team and of how much could be accomplished together. It was because of what I saw that day that I decided to accept that challenge and become a part of that team.

Leadership is one of the main keys to producing any program. To produce, you need someone who has the "game day" passion and who can lead people together in unison toward a single purpose. Someone needs to take the "bird's-eye view" of the program. Identifying this person, whom I'll call the producer, is the key step in producing a program. A producer is the point person who is there to make sure that the program stays on course—and to steer it back on course if needed. My suggestion is that the producer should not be involved in any of the program elements so that he or she can completely focus on the "big picture" and not just a small part of it.

How does the producer produce? When a program order is finally developed in the PDM, the producer can take specific steps to make the program happen. At Student Impact, our producers make time for three essential steps with every program they produce: (1) rehearsal; (2) talk-thru; and (3) run-thru. Let me explain.

The first step is to schedule rehearsals. God's intervention makes the ultimate difference in a person's life, but practice is one way we can be sure we are offering our best for the Lord. If you really want to improve your programs, then rehearsals must become a nonnegotiable part of the programming schedule.

To achieve excellence, those involved in the program need to rehearse individually or as a team what they will contribute. The vocalists and the band rehearse their songs. The drama team members memorize their lines and stage blocking. The message-giver recites his or her message and works on delivery and timing. The video and audio teams check the equipment to ensure its efficiency.

Once the rehearsals are completed, the producer is ready to gather the team for what we call talk-thru. A talk-thru is just what it sounds like: verbally talking through the order of each element in the program, which is shown on a cue sheet. Cue sheets list the exact order of the program and guide the programming team in keeping the program running smoothly.

# Student Impact Cue Sheet Overview

View as list

| | | |
|---|---|---|
| Date **11/18/88** | Speaker **Bo** | Title **Real Friends Stay** |
| Location **Auditorium** | Program **Impact** | Series **Real Friends** |

| Time | Element | Description |
|---|---|---|
| 5:00 | Rehearsal | 75 Minutes<br>band and vocals |
| 7:00 | Run-Thru | A full Run Thru - with all the elements present |
| 8:00 | Walk-In | Music on CD |
| 8:05 | Song | "You Got a Friend in Me" - Randy Newman<br>CD music |
| 8:10 | Video | "Real Friends Stick Together" scene - should be a light and fun clip that deals with a friendship<br>Any popular movie scene that is copyright approved and fits the purpose |
| 8:12 | Verbal | Series review<br>Jarrett Stevens - gives an overview of what has been learned and intros the next song |
| 8:15 | Song | "Don't Speak" by No Doubt<br>performed by Stephanie |
| 8:20 | Video | "Best Friends IV"<br>A video that has Melissa Horton, a high school student, talking about a friendship |
| 8:21 | Verbal | Topic Intro - story about friend sticking by her<br>Melissa Horton - a high school student telling a friend story |
| 8:24 | Song | "You've Got A Friend" by James Taylor<br>performed by Nate H. |
| 8:28 | Transition | Guitar reprise<br>play until Drama Team and props are on stage |
| 8:30 | Drama | "Real Friends?"<br>A drama monologue of a girl bitter about there being no Real Friends during tough times |
| 8:35 | Video | "A Real Friend Is . . ."<br>Students from different high schools answering what they feel are qualities of a Real Friend |
| 8:37 | Message | "Real Friends Stay"<br>Bo Boshers - The message will help students know the only Real Friend, Jesus Christ |
| 8:57 | Verbal | Announcements (next Impact & Insight series)<br>Bo Boshers - promotes the next ministry events |
| 9:00 | Walk-Out | A collection of contemporary Christian songs about friends<br>CD Music |

When you make up your own program cue sheets, try to include everything possible, from the lyrics of the songs to the message text (as much as the message-giver can provide). By using this tool, your team will be able to see both the "big picture" and the in-between elements, like prop transitions, monitor adjustments, etc., in the program. In addition cue sheets help those involved better understand how they fit into the program and what precedes and follows them. For instance, if a tender, reflective song precedes the message, the message-giver will know that starting his or her message off with a funny story may not be the best choice.

After talk-thru, the producer and his or her team are ready for the run-thru. Usually, run-thru occurs immediately before the actual program, although if you're new to the process you may want to schedule your run-thru a few days earlier to allow time for adjustments. A run-thru is like a dress rehearsal of the entire program from start to finish. The only element not gone through word-for-word is the message, unless other members of the team need specific cues from the message-giver. For example, if a message-giver needs a graphic to appear on the screen at a certain point in the message, he or she would need to agree on a cue with those operating the slides or video.

During a run-thru, the producer evaluates all the pieces of the program to make sure that, when they are put together, the program achieves the purpose you and your team decided on. Practically speaking, this means that producing will involve making decisions to cut, move, or adjust elements in order to fit the program's purpose. The producer might find that a song needs to be moved, a drama introduced, or a video shortened.

The producer should look for holes and unclear or empty elements—something missing in content or direction. I have found that unclear direction is the most common problem, so I often add a transition, which is a verbal statement of topical direction slotted in between or during elements to help the flow of the program and to add clarity.

Another common problem the producer should look for in a program are "islands" or "loose train cars." These are elements that seem all alone in content or direction or do not fit with where you want to take the program. The producer needs to imagine that the program elements form a series of train cars, connected together and moving toward one goal. When the producer identifies an island or loose train car, he or she can either connect it with a transition or cut it. Remember: The producer is orchestrating the whole evening, so it is his or her responsibility to make sure that every minute of every element counts.

Besides identifying potential program pitfalls, there are four ways the producer can be most effective. First, the producer must always be there. In order to have a clear picture of everything that is going to happen during the program, the producer may need to attend the rehearsals or early creative stages of as many program elements as possible so that he or she can steer the program in the proper direction. And the producer needs to lead the talk-thru and run-thru meetings so that he or she can intercept any possible glitches.

Second, the producer must also be honest. This will be the toughest part of his or her responsibility. Adjusting and sometimes cutting elements that people have spent many hours preparing is a difficult job. The producer needs to explain this possibility to his or her team prior to the program so that everyone understands the producer's role. There have been times that I had to make a choice to cut an element in a program even though there had been many hours put into rehearsing.

Third, the producer must be aggressive. This may seem a bit strange to some, but when dealing in a program environment, someone has to make decisions with confidence and quickness.

And fourth, the producer needs to be an encourager. Encouragement is the most effective way for a producer to build a team. The producer should try to be a "good finder." When someone on the team does something well, the producer should make sure to affirm and encourage this person. Catching people doing a task well or using their gifts as best they can is a great way to encourage. Being a good finder requires intentional effort by the producer, but will immensely benefit the members on the team.

After the program is over, a producer should be able to confidently walk out of the building after the program is over and feel that he or she and the team have given their best efforts to God. That is all He asks for. By God's grace, the Marks, Katies, Brians, Sarahs, and Kurts in the audience will, through the program, have encountered a picture of God that impacts their perspective forever.

*try this ...*

- If the role of producer is a new one for your ministry, use these tips to identify a good person for the job:

    In most cases, the program director (see the organizational chart in chapter 1) will serve as producer.

If you don't yet have a structure that includes a program director, but you are reading this book, chances are the most likely candidate for producer is you! But do go back to chapter 1 and work on building your team.

Remember that a producer is someone who can be there, be honest, be aggressive, and be an encourager.

- Before your run-thru, get a cue sheet and circle any areas of concern.
- Ask your team the following questions about each element. This will help both you and your team put into words what you are trying to accomplish with each time slot in the program.

What is the purpose of this element?
How does this element fit with the entire program?
Why is this element important to the program?

- During the program, carry a notebook to write down concerns, list follow-up phone calls needed, or just to take notes.
- Evaluate the logical flow of a program by running it past a few target students.
- Revisit your original purpose for the program and see if you are still on course.
- Watch the reaction of your team and others as they view the run-thru. This might reveal an unclear message or some areas of concern.
- Look for places that might need verbal transitions between elements to ensure clarity in your program.

*more resources*

Bennis, Warren. *On Becoming a Leader*. Reading, Mass.: Addison-Wesley Publishing Co., Inc., 1989.

Firestien, Roger L. *Leading on the Creative Edge*. Colorado Springs: Pinon Press, 1996.

Shula, Don and Ken Blanchard. *Everyone's a Coach*. Grand Rapids: Zondervan, 1995.

# pictures

## Start with your heart

**P**rayer is the programmer's greatest tool. It may seem like stating the obvious, but prayer is essential to the creative process. We do the work of planning and preparing, but it is only God who can take our efforts and gifts and produce life change. When we ask Him to inspire us and to have His way in the creative process, we will marvel at powerful programming "moments" that can only be explained by the work of the Holy Spirit.[1]

It's late at night and my house is still, except for the buzz of this hard drive. I'm sitting here trying to figure out one last way to motivate and encourage you to be purposeful in your programs. I want to challenge you to do everything possible to produce the best your ministry can so that students can grow deeper in their understanding of and love for God. If you have read this whole book, then you got the best picture I could give of a responsible process that can produce purposeful programs. But I realize that even this is not enough. Even though I shared what I have learned with you, I know I cannot change your heart. I believe your heart has to be consumed with passion for what you are doing, and I can't help you with that; only God can.

This week was a rough one for me, but there were moments from heaven that hit my soul and made what I do worth it all. My heart for God and for people grew larger. I experienced biblical community happening as students and leaders embraced a hurting team member. I witnessed three tear-filled high school seniors tell how God had changed their lives. I read a letter from a brother who is a returning prodigal. I looked over a room full of seeking high school students sitting, waiting for answers to their questions about life. I saw an idea come to life on the stage and in students' hearts. I was a part of God's work in people's lives as I participated in a New Testament type of ministry that changed my heart as much as it touched others.

It was worth it. Every heavenly encounter I experienced made my heart grow bigger. I realized that the busyness or pace of ministry won't ever change, but my heart can, if I look and listen for those God-given ministry moments. I encourage you to look for them, too!

My objective in this book was to share a process we use at Student Impact, a way to approach planning and preparing a program. I realize that what I have described is only one way to increase the chances for students to see an image of God and experience Him. Perhaps you need to change the order I have listed in this book, tear out a chapter, or create your own process. Whatever you need to do, I hope it has become clear to you that you need a process in place as you plan and develop programs. Whether we are programming for today's culture or tomorrow's, for busters or builders, for black or white, for big events or small group sessions, a purposeful process is the best shot we have at painting pictures of God for people to see.

Pictures are all around us. My home is full of them. We display them to show the defining moments in our lives. In 1972, my brother and I sat in our rooms at the foot of our beds, glued to our mother's side as she painted a picture of heaven and hell and God's plan for us. That picture was so clear to us that we both made decisions to follow Jesus Christ forever. In 1982, a football coach painted a picture of how God desired to use us for His purpose to build the church. That picture changed my life plans for good. In 1997, sitting in the back of our church, I listened to a former addict paint a picture of God's grace that changed his life for all of eternity.

My prayer is that this book will encourage and assist you and your team's programming efforts to hang in the hearts of those you lead a room full of heavenly pictures—pictures that will help them begin to understand and see an image of God.

# Notes

## Introduction

1. Stephen R. Covey, A. Roger Merrill, and Rebecca R. Merrill, *First Things First* (New York: Simon & Schuster, 1994).

2. *The American Heritage Dictionary of the English Language*, 3rd ed. (Boston: Houghton Mifflin Co., 1992).

## Step 1: Team

1. *The American Heritage Dictionary of the English Language*, 3rd ed. (Boston: Houghton Mifflin Co., 1992).

2. Jon Katzenbach and Douglas Smith, *The Wisdom of Teams* (New York: Harper Business, 1993), 45.

3. Stephen R. Covey, *Personal Leadership Application Workbook* (Provo, Utah: Covey Leadership Center, 1993), 5.

4. Stephen R. Covey, A. Roger Merrill, and Rebecca R. Merrill, *First Things First* (New York: Simon & Schuster, 1994), 198.

5. Kenneth Blanchard, *The One Minute Manager Builds High Performing Teams* (New York: William Morrow and Company, Inc., 1990), 25.

6. Thomas A. Kayser, *Building Team Power* (Burr Ridge, Ill.: Irwin Professional Publishing, 1994), 20.

7. Dietrich Bonhoeffer, *Life Together* (San Francisco: Harper & Row, 1954), 94.

8. Katzenbach and Smith, 23.

9. Warren Bennis and Burt Nanus, *Leaders* (New York: Harper & Row, 1985), 93.

10. John Maxwell, *Developing the Leaders Around You* (Nashville: Thomas Nelson, 1995), 37.

11. Phillip Keller, *Inspirational Writings* (New York: Inspirational Press, 1993), 289.

## Step 2: Plan

1. *The American Heritage Dictionary of the English Language*, 3rd ed. (Boston: Houghton Mifflin Co., 1992).

2. Robert M. Donnelly, *Guidebook to Planning* (New York: Van Nostrand Reinhold Company, 1984), vii.

3. Scott Dyer and Nancy Beach, *The Source* (Grand Rapids: Zondervan, 1996), 10.

4. Peter Drucker, *Managing the Non-Profit Organization* (New York: Harper Collins, 1990), 46.

5. Eugene B. Habecker, *Rediscovering the Soul of Leadership* (Wheaton, Ill.: Victor Books, 1996), 134–35.

6. Donnelly, ix.

**Step 3: Purpose**

1. *The American Heritage Dictionary of the English Language*, 3rd ed. (Boston: Houghton Mifflin Co., 1992).

2. Woody Hayes, as quoted by Glenn Van Ekeren, *Speaker's Sourcebook II* (Englewood Cliffs, N.J.: Prentice Hall, 1994), 301.

3. George Barna, *Generation Next* (Ventura, Calif.: Regal Books, 1995), 19.

4. Josh McDowell and Bob Hostetler, *Josh McDowell's Handbook on Counseling Youth* (Dallas: Word, 1996), 293.

5. G. Keith Olson, *Counseling Teenagers* (Loveland, Colo.: Group Books, 1984), 409.

6. Walt Mueller, *Understanding Today's Youth Culture* (Wheaton, Ill.: Tyndale, 1994), 264.

7. McDowell and Hostetler, 391.

8. Mueller, 268.

9. McDowell and Hostetler, 401.

10. Scott Dyer and Nancy Beach, *The Source* (Grand Rapids: Zondervan, 1996), 9.

11. George Barna, *The Frog in the Kettle* (Ventura, Calif.: Regal Books, 1990), 205.

12. Archbishop Fulton J. Sheen, as quoted by Edythe Draper, *Draper's Book of Quotations for the Christian World* (Wheaton, Ill.: Tyndale,1992), 616.

**Step 4: Target**

1. *The American Heritage Dictionary of the English Language*, 3rd ed. (Boston: Houghton Mifflin Co., 1992).

2. Gilbert Arland, as quoted by Edythe Draper, *Draper's Book of Quotations for the Christian World* (Wheaton, Ill.: Tyndale, 1992), 532.

3. Robert R. Brown, as quoted by Draper, 632.

## Step 5: Message

1. *Funk & Wagnall's Standard Encyclopedic College Dictionary* (New York: Funk & Wagnall's, 1968).

2. Leighton Ford, *The Power of Story* (Colorado Springs: NavPress, 1994), 116.

3. John Stott, *The Preacher's Portrait* (Grand Rapids: Eerdmans, 1961), 30.

4. Ford, 126.

5. Peter Kuzmic, as quoted by Edythe Draper, *Draper's Book of Quotations for the Christian World* (Wheaton, Ill.: Tyndale, 1992), 55.

6. Walt Mueller, *Understanding Today's Youth Culture* (Wheaton, Ill.: Tyndale, 1994), 126.

7. Mueller, 81.

8. Mueller, 132.

9. Mueller, 69.

10. Tim Celek and Dieter Zander, *Inside the Soul of a New Generation* (Grand Rapids: Zondervan, 1996), 81–82.

11. Ken Davis, *Secrets of Dynamic Communication* (Grand Rapids: Zondervan, 1991), 160–61.

12. Ford, 117.

13. Ford, 118.

## Step 6: Rationale

1. Stephen R. Covey, *The 7 Habits of Highly Effective People* (New York: Simon & Schuster, 1989), 98.

2. *Funk & Wagnall's Standard Encyclopedic College Dictionary* (New York: Funk & Wagnall's, 1968).

3. Ken Davis, *Secrets of Dynamic Communication* (Grand Rapids: Zondervan, 1991), 20, 51.

4. Harry Emerson Fosdick, as quoted by Edythe Draper, *Draper's Book of Quotations for the Christian World* (Wheaton, Ill.: Tyndale, 1992), 158.

5. Davis, 12.

6. Davis, 20.

## Step 7: Direction

1. *The American Heritage Dictionary of the English Language*, 3rd ed. (Boston: Houghton Mifflin Co., 1992).

2. Scott Dyer and Nancy Beach, *The Source* (Grand Rapids: Zondervan, 1996), 13.

3. Dyer and Beach, 13.

4. Stephen R. Covey, *The 7 Habits of Highly Effective People* (New York: Simon & Schuster, 1989), 95.

**Step 8: Ideas**

1. *Funk & Wagnall's Standard Encyclopedic College Dictionary* (New York: Funk & Wagnall's, 1968).

2. Albert Szent-Gyorgyi, as quoted by Roger von Oech, *A Whack on the Side of the Head* (New York: Warner Books, 1990), 7.

3. Charles "Chic" Thompson, *What A Great Idea!* (New York: Harper Perennial, 1992), 4.

4. Glenn Van Ekeren, *Speaker's Sourcebook II* (Englewood Cliffs, New Jersey: Prentice Hall, 1994), 85, 206.

5. Oliver Wendell Holmes, as quoted by Thompson, *What a Great Idea!*, 6.

6. von Oech, 10.

7. Ken Davis, *How to Speak to Youth* (Loveland, Colo.: Group Books, 1986), 17–18.

8. Ted Engstrom, as quoted by Van Ekeren, *Speaker's Sourcebook II*, 80.

9. Gloria Hoffman and Pauline Graivier, as quoted by Van Ekeren, *Speaker's Sourcebook II*, 79.

10. Dr. Yoshiro Nakamats, as quoted by Thompson, *What a Great Idea!*, xiv.

11. Thompson, 12.

12. Michael Eisner, "Managing a Creative Organization: Never Being Afraid to Fail," *Vital Speeches of the Day* (June 1, 1996), 2:502.

13. Scott Dyer and Nancy Beach, *The Source* (Grand Rapids: Zondervan, 1996), 14.

14. von Oech, 38.

**Step 9: Resources**

1. *The American Heritage Dictionary of the English Language*, 3rd ed. (Boston: Houghton Mifflin Co., 1992).

2. Roger von Oech, *A Kick in the Seat of the Pants* (New York: Harper Perennial, 1986), 28.

3. Glenn Van Ekeren, *Speaker's Sourcebook II* (Englewood Cliffs, New Jersey: Prentice Hall, 1994), 80.

**Step 10: Develop**

1. Martin Holden, *The Encyclopedia of Gemstones and Minerals* (New York: Michael Friedman Publishing Group, 1991), 193.

2. *The American Heritage Dictionary of the English Language*, 3rd ed. (Boston: Houghton Mifflin Co., 1992).

3. Edythe Draper, *Draper's Book of Quotations for the Christian World* (Wheaton, Ill.: Tyndale, 1992), 295.

4. Roger L. Firestien, *Leading on the Creative Edge* (Colorado Springs: Pinon Press, 1996), 10.

**Step 11: Produce**

1. *Funk & Wagnall's Standard Encyclopedic College Dictionary* (New York: Funk & Wagnall's), 1968.

2. Edythe Draper, *Draper's Book of Quotations for the Christian World* (Wheaton, Ill.: Tyndale, 1992), 475.

3. Josh McDowell and Bob Hostetler, *Right From Wrong* (Dallas: Word Publishing, 1994), 6.

4. Carol Anderson, as quoted by Roger L. Firestien, *Leading on the Creative Edge* (Colorado Springs: Pinon Press, 1996), 19.

**Conclusion**

1. Scott Dyer and Nancy Beach, *The Source* (Grand Rapids: Zondervan, 1996), 352.

# STUDENT

# IMPACT

Over twenty years ago, God gave a vision to a group of high school students to reach out to their non-Christian friends in a purposeful and creative way and share with them God's love. This vision to reach lost people helped build a vibrant student ministry from which Willow Creek Community Church was formed.

Today, that vision lives on in Student Impact, the high school ministry of Willow Creek, as high school students continue to reach their friends for Christ. Student Impact's mission is to help nonbelieving high school students become fully devoted followers of Jesus Christ. With a student core and small group participation of five hundred, over one thousand students have attended the weekly outreach program and lives continue to be changed.

To find out more about Student Impact, you can

- Attend the Student Impact Leadership Conference (SILC) held each May, which includes corporate teaching times and a wide range of pertinent seminars taught by youth leaders. For more information write or call the Willow Creek Association at

  P.O. Box 3188
  Barrington, IL 60011–3188
  (847) 765–0070

- Visit WIN City, Student Impact's web page on the Internet. You will find an idea factory, a resource museum, a news house, and a network village designed to equip you with resources. Check the Willow Creek Association's web page (www.willowcreek.org.) for a link.
- Investigate Student Impact's two-year internship for men and women interested in hands-on student ministry experience. Call the Student Impact office for more information: (847) 765–5029.

Additional Student Impact resources are available through Zondervan.

# WILLOW CREEK
## RESOURCES

*This resource was created to serve you.*

It is just one of many ministry tools that are part of the Willow Creek Resources® line, published by the Willow Creek Association together with Zondervan Publishing House. The Willow Creek Association was created in 1992 to serve a rapidly growing number of churches from all across the denominational spectrum that are committed to helping unchurched people become fully devoted followers of Christ. There are now more than 2,500 WCA member churches worldwide.

The Willow Creek Association links like-minded leaders with each other and with strategic vision, information, and resources in order to build prevailing churches. Here are some of the ways it does that:

• **Church Leadership Conferences**—3 1/2-day events, held at Willow Creek Community Church in South Barrington, IL, that are being used by God to help church leaders find new and innovative ways to build prevailing churches that reach unchurched people.

• *The Leadership Summit*—a once-a-year event designed to increase the leadership effectiveness of pastors, ministry staff, volunteer church leaders, and Christians in business.

• **Willow Creek Resources®**—to provide churches with a trusted channel of ministry resources in areas of leadership, evangelism, spiritual gifts, small groups, drama, contemporary music, and more. For more information, call Willow Creek Resources® at 800/876-7335. Outside the US call 610/532-1249.

• *WCA News*—a bimonthly newsletter to inform you of the latest trends, resources, and information on WCA events from around the world.

• *The Exchange*—our classified ads publication to assist churches in recruiting key staff for ministry positions.

• **The Church Associates Directory**—to keep you in touch with other WCA member churches around the world.

• *WillowNet*—an Internet service that provides access to hundreds of Willow Creek messages, drama scripts, songs, videos, and multimedia suggestions. The system allows users to sort through these elements and download them for a fee.

• *Defining Moments*—a monthly audio journal for church leaders, in which Lee Strobel asks Bill Hybels and other Christian leaders probing questions to help you discover biblical principles and transferable strategies to help maximize your church's potential.

For conference and membership information please write or call:

Willow Creek Association　　　　　　ph: (847) 765-0070
P.O. Box 3188　　　　　　　　　　　fax: (847) 765-5046
Barrington, IL 60011-3188　　　　　　www.willowcreek.org

We want to hear from you. Please send your comments about this
book to us in care of the address below. Thank you.

**ZondervanPublishingHouse**
*Grand Rapids, Michigan 49530*
http://www.zondervan.com